Mantra&
Meditation

Superconscious Meditation, Volume 2

Mantra &
Meditation

Superconscious Meditation, Volume 2

Pandit Usharbudh Arya, D.Litt.

Published by

HIMALAYAN INTERNATIONAL INSTITUTE
OF YOGA SCIENCE & PHILOSOPHY
OF THE U.S.A.

Honesdale, Pennsylvania

© 1981 by The Himalayan International Institute
of Yoga Science and Philosophy of the U.S.A.
RR 1, Box 400
Honesdale, Pennsylvania 18431

06 05 04 03 02 01 00 99 98 97 96   7 6 5 4

The paper used in this publication meets the minimum requirements
of the American National Standard for Information Sciences—
Permanence of Paper for Printed Library Materials, ANSI Z39.48-
1984. ♾

Library of Congress Catalog Card Number: 81-84076
ISBN: 0-89389-074-X

Acknowledgements

I wish to thank sincerely the Board of Directors and close friends of the Center for Higher Consciousness for having made it possible for me to cancel some of my travels to finish the writing of this book.

Also, my gratitude goes to Professor Ronald Neuhaus of the University of Wisconsin at River Falls for editing the subject order and general plan of the book and to the editors of the Himalayan Institute for their careful and strenuous work of editing.

Thanks are also due to Mary Gail Sovik and her team of Center members for their hard work in typing the several drafts of the book and to the Bjustroms for in-depth proofreading.

In this work, whatever is beneficial comes from the Guru lineage and whatever is faulty is mine.

All the Deities live by the Word,
By the Word also the celestial dancers and the humans;
All these worlds are deposited in the Word—
May that Word, the Consort of the Masterful King of heavens,
Indra, hear our calling. For—
The Word is the imperishable first-born of the Law and Truth,
The Mother of Vedas, the navel of Immortality (Amrta).

Taittiriya Brahmana II.8.8.5

Gurudeva,
    Yours
    to you.

Foreword

The Practice of Meditation

There are two ways to state the nature of an object or an experience: to define what it is, or to refute what it is not. Many philosophers and saints of the East and West, such as Buddha, Shankara and Meister Eckhardt, have emphasized the latter method in describing God and mystical or meditative experiences. Because the meditational experience is not available to many, it is very easy to mislead people about its nature by making false statements concerning it. Such statements and misconceptions are found in abundance. Let us examine and clarify a few of these.

One of the misconceptions is that meditation is a dangerous emptying of the mind, leaving it open to the invasion of all kinds of devils. On the contrary, meditation is a stilling of the mind, bringing it peace and tranquility. It is not merely an emptying—peace is peace and not just an absence of war; silence is not simply an absence of words; stillness is not an absence of energy. The average mind is habituated to remain constantly agitated and out of this agitation develop most of our problems and many of our mental and physical illnesses. It is impossible to soothe the mind by adding to it agitating experiences, or more objects, or even by rational analysis because, whether rationally or emotionally, the mind in such cases continues to spin like a top.

What, then, is the best way for the mind to be brought to peace? Imagine yourself working as a mother in the kitchen. Your back is turned, and your eighteen-month-old toddler comes from behind you, picks up a sharp knife by its edge, and holds it lightly in his fist. How can you persuade him to drop the knife? The glittering blade attracts him, and he regards it as his possession. You cannot pull it out of his hand, nor can you argue with him. You are in a dilemma. But there is in your mind a faculty called *sattva,* the purer aspect of your being, which comes alive in spite of all the agitation *(rajas)* that you are feeling at that moment. *Sattva* is awakened because love is present. In the light of that *sattva,* a mother finds a way, and she draws the child's attention to something shiny in red, blue or yellow colors and offers it to him. The child drops the knife and extends his palm. You can take the knife away from him, but only by replacing it with something else more attractive. Similarly, the mind will not easily loosen its grip on the object of its attraction; its habit of agitation and excitation cannot be suddenly changed. It must be offered some other thought upon which it can concentrate. The mantra in meditation is that thought which replaces the knife's cutting edge of all rational and emotional associations so that the mind may come to a center.

Many people ask, "Why do I need a mantra? Why can I not meditate on love?" The answer is that you may certainly do so, but how do you define that love on which you would meditate? How would you ascertain that you were indeed meditating on pure love that is not alloyed with attachments, expectations, jealousies and even outright hatred? How many human beings have indeed experienced love which is unbounded, unlimited and directed towards all living beings in the whole universe? Until one has experienced such love, any meditation on love is alloyed; it will only lead to strengthening the dichotomy of opposites in emotion. The thought of love will bring the thought of hate or the thought of someone you love very much and of someone else whom you love very little. In this way, the total balance of the mind will be disturbed within a few short moments. But if you have already experienced the unbounded universal love, then you have transcended the need for meditation. Such unbounded love flows only from the very pure, the few rare masters who have attained such status.

Others ask, "Why can I not meditate on God?" Unfortunately, much of the time we do not meditate on God, nor do we pray to God, but we address our prayers merely to our notions of God. But God says—"I have nothing to do with your notions of me; I am far beyond them." So first, we must remove the veils we have placed on our God-seeing inner eye. The process of meditation is that of removing these veils. The distracted mind is brought to focus on a mantra so that the power of negative thoughts may be reduced. As the mind centers on the mantra, other thoughts and emotions that stood in the way of the individual soul witnessing the light of God gradually diminish and finally vanish.

Many people imagine meditation to be comparable to dreams and fantasies, but the comparison is completely misplaced because in a dream, *one becomes many,* whereas in meditation, *many become one.* Let us elaborate. The person who is dreaming is one. In the dream he sees someone coming towards him and finally attacking him. He sees a crowd of a thousand spectators gathering, watching the spectacle of the fight between himself and the assailant. The question arises, who is the assailant and who are the thousand spectators? In his waking hours he has faced many conflicts which he has suppressed, and in the dream the suppressed conflicts show up in the form of such jousts. In his waking hours, he has craved to share his inner conflicts with a thousand people, and in the dream the wish is fulfilled. Again, the question remains: Who is his assailant and who are the spectators? They all are fragments of his mind, taking on, as it were, independent personalities, but it is he himself who has become many.

In wakeful hours, we put on the garb of many different and conflicting personalities, but in meditation, all of these assumptions of different personalities and thoughts, emotions and disturbances, subside. Only the continuity of a single meditative thought remains, which is the mantra. The random thoughts continue to arise during meditation, however, because the mind continues to pull a meditator towards the objects of the world, to which he is habituated.

Often the pattern of thoughts arising is a dreamlike one, giving vent to many subconscious impulses, memories, desires and cravings. Those whose meditation has not yet reached its utmost possible maturity often imagine that they receive messages from other worlds, other planes, other times and places during meditation. Many have written books purporting them to be messages from masters of Tibet or ancient Egypt! These are all alloyed thoughts, and some of them may even come from the depths of the subconscious mind where they become mixed with all kinds of personal ambitions, egos and one's own world view. Ask the masters of the Himalayas, and they will openly state that no such messages were given! Until the meditator's mind reaches absolute purity, it must not move from the concentration on the mantra, otherwise one is subject to take all of one's imagination—conscious or unconscious— seriously, and be led away from the main track.

The same advice applies to those who undertake the practice of meditation in order to become mind-readers and psychics. People have great fascination for this ability, but they also have great misunderstanding of it. In one particular country, I was invited to lecture at the Police Training Academy and the sponsors had hoped that I would teach them how they could find criminals mentally through meditation and then apprehend them! In another instance, a caller once asked the staff at the Center for Higher Consciousness in Minneapolis whether we taught courses in mind reading. After some futile exchanges on the phone, the members of the Center referred the caller to me. He asked me the same question: "Do you teach courses in mind reading?"

I replied, "Yes, I do." He was all excited and wanted to know the times and dates of the next course. I gave him the information on my next course, Superconscious Meditation. Then he asked, "Do you mean that after taking a few weeks' course I will be able to read minds?" I said, "Indeed, starting with your own!" People want to read everybody else's mind but their own. Is not the confusion of one's own mind enough that he would not want to invade the privacy of others' minds and gather their confusion to add to his own? You do not want to read other people's mail, why do you wish to read their minds?

Some people similarly claim to have the power of astral travel, whatever that means. The statement normally goes something like this: "I was in my bedroom in Minneapolis, and then I felt something go out of my skull; it was my own astral body. I reached the room of my sister, who lives in California, and found that she had gone to bed wearing blue pajamas." Nowadays, a simple phone call would have been sufficient! One does not need to practice meditation for such advancements. The aim and purpose for which one is undertaking the practice of meditation must be very pure and not a pursuit of powers. The same applies to the ability to predict the future. If you make a hundred predictions, by the law of averages, perhaps fifty will come true. It is then very simple to call up the best public relations firm and have yourself declared a prophet and go to press all over the country. But what is the end result of all this dabbling in prophecies and predictions except satisfaction of one's own ego? In meditation ego is replaced by concentration on mantra.

Sometimes meditation teachers are asked about the truth of sciences such as palmistry and astrology. People ask "Can you read my palm? What is going to happen to me, dear astrologer? Can you predict my future? Will I marry a rich person? Will I have the girl of my desire? Will I be wealthy, famous, successful? Will my desires be fulfilled?"

All these questions are expressions of our emotional insecurities. If my life is run by the stars, by whom is the life of the stars run? A meditator goes direct to that source which controls all the stars of all the universes. Or, if he must depend on himself, then he aims at fulfilling his own *karma* and accepts the results of his past *karma*. He waits for the fruits of seeds previously sown to fructify and meanwhile remains at peace. Anxieties and insecurities are not for him.

This is not to say that there is no truth to the sciences of palmistry or astrology, but many of the predictions based on these may not come true because human volition is a most powerful force that can change the course and momentum of the fruition of one's *karma*. A meditator is a person of action, and he directs the action of his mind, speech and body with great wisdom. Throughout his daily life he maintains the concentration on his *karma* to replace his anxieties and insecurities.

This is as far as one should go in his interest in palmistry, astrology or other sciences of prediction. Just as the pursuit of astral travel and predictions of personal future are meaningless for a meditator, so also are the prophecies concerning the impending end of the world, or statements that we are living in a new age or that a new age is about to dawn. The universe runs in cycles—there is creation after dissolution and dissolution after each creation. This particular moment is the end of all previous moments. Any new age dawning must dawn within the individual mind and not by some divine decree for which later generations may blame the creator. A meditator in today's scientific world cannot be interested in foreclosing the world and dropping out of his community to form some little commune, some utopia or some other new age. Let a dawn of light appear within his own mind. When the mind is focused single-pointedly on the mantra, it is centered on this particular moment, on here and now, not trembling at the prospects of the world ending the day after tomorrow, nor excited at some special happening that will change the course of civilization overnight, or in a year, without any effort for self-purification on the part of each individual.

Some people practice their mantras to gain *siddhis* or supernatural powers, but according to the yoga system, all powers are natural ones, and there are no supernatural powers. To illustrate: once upon a time I had a cat. This was a very intelligent cat. Everyone's cat is very intelligent, as we all know. But my cat was really super-intelligent, and if it was in a room with the door closed, it would try to reach up and turn the knob with its forepaws. Of course it could not succeed, so it would look at me as though to say, "Meow—would you please open this door?"

I would extend my hand, turn the knob and open the door. The cat would walk out, turn its neck and say to me, "Meow—thank you, you have supernatural powers!" My very natural hands seemed supernatural to the cat because she could not turn a doorknob with her paws.

According to the Yoga Sutras of Patanjali, the practice of meditation *adds* no special powers at all. All the powers are always present within us, but they are lying blocked *(Sutra IV.3)*. When a farmer wants to irrigate his field, he does not create water, nor does he push it into the field. He simply raises the sluice gate that was blocking the flow, and the field is automatically irrigated. The blocks we have placed in our minds are simply removed in meditation so that the inner forces begin to function, and all our faculties come to their fullest possible growth. To others who have not yet learned to remove these blocks that are in the way of their innate power, a yogi's use of such powers appears supernatural. As the practitioner, the *sadhaka,* improves in his practice of meditation, however, he begins to sense the presence of these special faculties, which for many incarnations he had permitted to atrophy. Yet this rediscovery of faculty after hidden faculty can in fact become an impediment, and often is, in the way of the fullest spiritual development. Their presence may be exciting in the state of wakefulness, but on the path to ultimate meditation, *samadhi,* they are indeed blocks and impediments. *(Sutra III.36).* It is for this reason that a *sadhaka* is discouraged by the master from using these powers except by his specific permission, in utmost secret so as not to advertize them for the sake of ego, and only for the benefit of others. The temptation to be a Rasputin comes easily, but the aspiration to become a master is very difficult. Even though there are special mantras for the unfoldment of these powers, in a life busy with so many distractions and so little time available for pure meditation, one is better advised not to waste time using these mantras but to remain true to the practice of one's own personal mantra.

There is a story that illustrates this. It occurs in the literature of all the spiritual traditions in different forms attributed to different masters. Here we give the Buddhist version:

> Once upon a time, a very proud man came in the presence of the Buddha and boasted that he could walk on water. The Buddha appeared very impressed and asked, "How long did it take you to

master this power?" The man replied with a haughty air, "A full twelve years!" The Buddha said, "Which way did you come here?" The man told him that he had to cross the river just now, and he did so by just walking over the water. The Buddha seemed worried: "I have to go that way tomorrow, but I do not walk on water. How will I cross the river?" "Well," the man said, "You will have to pay five pennies to the boatman." The Buddha laughed and said, "My dear man, did you say that it took you twelve years to master the power of walking on the water?" The man replied, "Indeed, yes." The Buddha laughed and said, "Why would I waste twelve years on something accomplished by paying five pennies?"

A similar story occurs in Swami Rama's *Living with the Himalayan Masters,** about a swami who could produce fire from his mouth. It had taken him twenty years to master this, and Swami Rama's master told him, "A match will produce fire in a second. If you wish to spend twenty years to produce fire from your mouth, you are a fool." All these pursuits of powers are instruments of ego, and they are no better than the desire to become a millionaire, a king, a politician or a high government official! When such desires arise in your mind, simply concentrate on the vibration of the mantra and let no other ambitions intervene.

Some misinformed persons have tried to associate the practice of meditation with the cult of drugs. There can be no two experiences as opposed to each other as that of drugs and that of meditation. Under the influence of such substances as LSD, marijuana or mushrooms of various kinds, the mind is under control of something that has been introduced externally. In meditation, the mind is totally self-controlled. One is a

* Swami Rama, *Living with the Himalayan Masters*. Honesdale, Pa: Himalayan Institute, 1980, p. 106

dependency; the other is freedom. One is *tamas,* a darkening of the mind and a throwing of many more layers of veils on the faculties of light, intuition and wisdom; the other is a lifting of those veils to free the light of *sattva,* harmony, so that the eyes of wisdom might open.

A mind under the influence of drugs is not capable of directing itself or of responding to the volition of free spirit, but in meditation it is free of all preconditions and is not being conditioned to anything external from the world of objects. The influence of drugs is on the brain, the influence of meditation is on the mind. When the brain is being chemically directed towards random thoughts and feelings over which one has no control, the mind at the same time cannot be directed to meditate. A mind under the influence of drugs is, therefore, not capable of concentration on any object, including the mantra. Meditation, on the other hand begins with concentration on the mantra.

Meditation is also being put in the same class as experiments on sensory deprivation. As was said in *Superconscious Meditation,** every internal experience is not the experience of the eternal transcendental. The confusion between the experiments of sensory deprivation and meditation arises from the shallow understanding of meditation as merely a blocking of the flow of stimuli through the senses into the mind.

It must be understood that the mind has many sources of input. One source, of course, is the stimuli coming in through the senses and the nuero-cerebral system, but the surfaces of the mind also receive stimulation in the form of thought patterns, fantasies, emotions and dreams that arise from memories recorded within the subconscious mind. In other words, every thought, feeling and emotion that arises in the mind is not simply an output from the deeper surfaces but is at the same

* Arya, Pandit U., *Superconscious Meditation.* Honesdale, Pa: Himalayan Institute, 1978

time also an input. The mind remembers everything that has ever happened in the physical body, even at the cellular level, from the moment of conception. Every cellular change, in other words, is recorded in the mind because the energy of the mind permeates every particle of the physical body. Similarly, everything that has ever happened, however minute, in the internal organs, in the flow of hormones, in the glands, in the nerves and muscles, in the skin and in every pore is recorded by the mind.

It is well known that every input from the senses is stored in the memory, but what is most often forgotten is that every thought, feeling and emotion, even though unexpressed, remains in the memory of the mind. If it were not so, how would we ever say, "I dreamt," "I thought so at such and such a time, " "I felt this way in such a situation"? *Each time the memory of a thought, feeling or emotion is remembered, it immediately becomes a fresh input.* If no external stimuli were ever introduced into the mind, the undercurrents of the subconscious and the unconscious would continue to send forth tides, waves, ripples and bubbles to the surface of the mind.

This is what happens in dreams, hallucinations and fantasies. The mind creates a closed circuit—each image is fed back, gathers force, picks up many past residues, and forms a fresh image—and the vicious circle continues. These images are similarly produced in any kind of sensory deprivation, but this is not the way of freedom from the slavery of the subconscious and the unconscious mind.

Those who have not understood the nature of meditation as a controlled smooth flow of mind within a single channel mistake the hallucinations of sensory deprivation as mystic experiences. But the mystics of all ages and religions were always warned that when they withdrew into the deserts and the caves they must not allow these 'messengers of the devil' to penetrate the mind. The Christian mystics were advised to maintain the mind on prayer, and the yogis are advised to maintain the mind on mantra. The practices analogous to sensory deprivation are well known to the yoga tradition. The disciple spends days, weeks, months and years in caves or closed cells where not even the picture of angels or deities or natural scenes are allowed, and the mind must dwell only on a single object of concentration. This is the important point: the mind must dwell on a single object of concentration. It must be given a way of establishing internal control so that uncontrolled imageries cease to flow and diffuse energy. Until the mind has something internal like a mantra, a forced withdrawal of the senses from the world of objects and a simulation of a withdrawal of the mind from the world of senses will only lead to the strengthening of hallucinogenic tendencies. These tendencies create further blocks on the way to spiritual progress. They are additional waves of *rajas,* the quality of restlessness in nature and in the mind. In the states of sensory deprivation an empty mind, without a mantra, could eventually be led to destructive tendencies.

But in any case, such a mind is not really being opened inwards to the pure self as defined in the yoga system of philosophy and as explained in Chapters II and III of *Superconscious Meditation.* In this context we repeat our earlier assertion that meditation is not an emptying of the mind; it is a dynamic fullness. The yogi reaches into the mind's depths and brings out energies to direct his personality anew, sending forth the beams of the same energy for the guidance, healing and enlightenment of others. All the other above-mentioned pursuits and states that are misconceived as meditation are tricks of the ego, and a true pursuer of the path of purification is not trapped in the ego's nets. Let us understand the difference between the pursuit of ego and that of meditation:

- The infinite in the finite, mistaking itself to be finite, is ego.
- The infinite in the finite, knowing itself to be infinite, is meditation.
- The mantra is the thread from the finite leading to the infinite and, in deep meditation, bringing the presence of the infinite into the finite.
- The finite, here, is the external end of the personality such as the physical body, and the infinite is the pure self. The link between the finite and the infinite is the mind.

Contents

Introduction

by
Sri Swami Rama

Mantra and Meditation is a book that will dispel the darkness of ignorance of many students who are confused. This book can lead to an understanding, knowledge and an ability to practice the science of meditation. When a meditator probes into the inner levels of his being exploring the unknown dimensions of interior life, he needs a systematic and scientific method which can lead him to the next state of experience. Then, he can go beyond all the levels of his unconscious mind and establish himself in his essential nature.

From childhood onward, we are taught to examine and understand things in the external world, but nobody teaches us to look within and understand the mind and its various states. A human being, after examining the objects of the external world, finds that he has not yet understood and known himself or his internal states. Anyone who has examined the objects of the external world and their transitory nature understands that life has more to give and then he starts searching within himself. In order to do research in the interior world, we have to apply an exact science if we really want to know the center of

Consciousness hidden deep in the inner recesses of our being. Many students out of curiosity or excitement are turning toward meditative methods and trying to understand them as means of knowing their internal states. Some of these students persist and others give up exploring their inner dimensions.

In this book, Dr. U. Arya explains that all the existing spiritual traditions of the world use a syllable, a sound, a word or set of words called Mantra as a bridge to cross the mire of delusion and go to the other shore of life. *Mantra Setu* is that which helps the meditator make the mind one-pointed, inward, and then, finally leads to the center of Consciousness, the deep recesses of eternal silence where peace, happiness and bliss reside.

Many spiritual traditions have somehow, somewhere already lost this science of mantra. They remain scratching the surface in the external world, just muttering a certain few words in their own language which they call a prayer.

Prayer definitely purifies the way of soul, but the method of meditation is a systematized way of exploring the interior self and inner states of human life. There is a vast difference between prayer and meditation. Prayer is a petition to someone with a particular desire to be fulfilled while the method of meditation leads one from his gross self to the subtlemost self. Those who are students of life can clearly understand the difference between prayer and meditation. Prayer, meditation and contemplation are different tools, different ways for attaining the goal of life.

It is clear that the method of meditation is not any ritual belonging to any particular religion, culture or group. Our tradition is a meditative tradition which does not oppose any religion or culture, but teaches one to systematically explore the inner dimensions. Many Westerners are scared of the word meditation and say that this is an Eastern tradition, forgetting that *The Bible* clearly says, "Be still and know that I am God."

How to be still is the method of meditation. Even to imitate the way others are meditating is very relaxing. Meditation is beneficial for physical, mental and spiritual health.

In meditation, one has to learn to be still first. This begins with a physical stillness. First, the student is guided by a competent teacher to keep his head, neck and trunk straight. According to the tradition that we follow, *asana* or the meditative posture is carefully selected according to the nature and capacity of the student. It is not changed, but one posture is accomplished. After accomplishing stillness with the help of the meditative posture, the student understands the obstacles arising from muscle twitching, tremors occurring in various parts of the body, shaking and itching.

These obstacles arise from lack of discipline because the body has never been trained to be placed in a still position. We are trained to move in the external world faster and faster, but nobody trains us how to be still. For being still, an orderly habit should be found and, for forming this habit, one should learn to be regular and punctual in practicing the same posture, at the same time and at the same place until the body habits stop rebelling against the discipline given to it. This primary step, though very basic, is very important. It should not be ignored. Otherwise the student will not be able to reap the desired fruits and his efforts will be wasted.

We should learn about mantra and meditation by studying only those books which have been written by the meditators and should avoid the trash literature written for commercial use. A book definitely guides and inspires the student, but, finally, the book of life seems to be the most important. The highest of all books is the book of life. Meditators and contemplators alone can unfold the pages of this book.

Contemplation and meditation are two different words and methods. Meditation is a definite method like a ladder having many rungs which finally leads to the roof from where one can see the vast horizon above, below, here, there and everywhere. Contemplation also uses a systematic method of examining the principles of life and the universe, constantly assimilating these ideas and transforming the whole personality. Those who are fully dedicated and have given their whole life for self-realization use both methods—meditation in deep silence and contemplation in daily life. Contemplation is seeking and searching for truth and meditation is practicing and experiencing truth.

The Lord of Life is truth. Let us practice truth with mind, action and speech. Secondly, Love is the Light of Lights. Let us radiate this love by not hurting, harming, injuring and killing others. Such ideas if practiced in daily life are called contemplation.

We believe that all great religions have come from one and the same reality. We also believe that without knowing the absolute truth, the purpose of life cannot be accomplished.

Though the schools of meditation and contemplation are two different schools, they both can help a student go beyond and establish himself in his essential nature. Our essential nature is peace, happiness and bliss. It is the mind that stands as a wall between apparent reality and absolute reality. Mantra is a means, meditation is a method, and the constant state of awareness of absolute truth is the attainment that fulfills the purpose of life.

This method of meditation is an inner method which has been thoroughly explored for centuries together by the great sages. There are various channels of knowledge, knowledge through the mind, knowledge through the senses, knowledge through instinct, but the finest of all is the intuitive knowledge which has been the guide of all great men in the past. To reach this infinite library within is not so easy; it is a difficult task, but it is not impossible. As a scholar works hard to accomplish his task in any academic field, the meditator should also collect the data from various traditions and examine the methods before he applies a particular method suitable to him. So often the students talk only of this method and that method, and they get confused by the sayings and writings of modern writers and speakers.

The meditative scholars instruct the student in how to be free from the external influences, and how to follow the primary steps so that body, senses and mind are prepared for meditative experiences. If these preliminaries are ignored, then the student might waste years and years in hallucination and fantasy just to feed his ego and not have any valid experiences. A valid experience is the experience which guides the student. A human being has experiences on many levels, but all experiences do not guide him. A valid experience is so clear that he does not need any external evidence to support that experience. Such an experience is gained only when the student attains a state of equanimity and tranquility.

As a student makes sincere efforts to find a right teacher and a suitable method of meditation, so actually a teacher also remains in search of a good student who is fully prepared to take this voyage—the voyage from the known to the unknown. Doubts and fears may arise on various occasions, but when the student decides to tread the path of meditation, he honestly prepares and disicplines himself. He examines all his instrumentation in the laboratory of life. Body, senses, breath and mind are attuned toward meditation only.

Those who have been researchers and have examined the external joys find that the highest of all joys is meditation, and this joy leads to that eternal joy called *samadhi*. Such great ones like to keep their eyes partially closed, peeping into the innermost light that shines within this frame of life.

According to our tradition, which is purely a meditative tradition more than five thousand years old, mantra and meditation are inseparable just like two sides of a coin. Some of the shallow methods which have been taught lead one only so far, but the systematic method which is explained in this book can help a student to attain the highest of all states. For practicing the method of meditation, one should not dive into shallow waters for the pearls of life are found in the deep ocean of life and not in the ponds, lakes and rivers.

During deep meditation, the great sages heard certain sounds which were called mantras. In *The Bible,* it is said that those who have an ear to hear will hear. When the mind becomes attuned, it becomes capable of hearing the voice of the unknown. The sounds which are heard in such a state do not belong to any particular language, religion or tradition.

There are two types of sounds. The sounds which are created by the external world and heard by the ears are different than the sounds heard in deep meditation; such sounds are called *anahata nada*—the sound of drums without drums. Inner sounds which are heard in deep meditation by the sages do not vibrate exactly like sound vibrates in the external world. These inner sounds have a leading quality. They lead the meditator towards the center of silence within. The following simile can help in understanding this: imagine that you are standing on the bank of a river and you hear the current as it flows. If you follow the river upstream, you will come to its origin. There you will find that there is no sound. In the same way, a mantra leads the mind to the silence within. That state is called "soundless sound."

The mantra imparted by a teacher to a student is not at all a commercial proposition. It is more like a prescription given to a patient. There are innumerable sounds, each with different affects. The teacher must find out which best suits a particular student according to his/her attitudes, emotions, desires and habits.

A mantra has four bodies or *koshas* (sheaths). First, as a

word, it has a meaning; another more subtle form is its feeling; still more subtle is a deep intense and constant awareness or presence, and the fourth or most subtle level of the mantra is soundless sound.

Many students continue repeating or muttering their mantra throughout life, but they never attain a state of *ajapa japa*—that state of constant awareness without any effort. Such a student strengthens his awareness, but meditates on the gross level only.

The mantras which are used for meditation in silence are special sets of sounds which do not obstruct and disturb the flow of breath, but help regulate the breath and lead to *sushumna* awakening where breath flows from both nostrils equally. This is a state where the breath and mind function in complete harmony. Application of *sushumna* is a joyous state of mind. After attaining this state the mind is voluntarily disconnected from the dissipation of the senses. Then the student has to deal with the thoughts coming forward from the storehouse of merits and demerits—the unconscious mind. It is a vast reservoir where we all store impressions of our lifetime. The conscious mind is in the habit of recalling these memories from the deep levels of the unconscious. Mantra helps one to go beyond this process. Mantra creates a new groove and the mind begins to spontaneously flow into the groove created by mantra. When the mind becomes concentrated, one-pointed and inward, it peers into the latent part of the unconscious and there sooner or later finds a glittering light.

The most important role that mantra plays is during the transition period that every human being has to go through. A dying man wants to communicate with his loved ones. The attachment that we create for the mortal things and people produce serious and painful troubles for a dying man. For lack of philosophy, which ought to have been built during his lifetime, for lack of practice of meditation and self-experience, attachments become very painful. Death itself is not painful, but the fear of death is very painful especially for those who have not pondered over the mystery of birth, death and the hereafter. In such cases, these last moments of life cause extreme discomfort and even affect the voyage after death. This subtle observation leads me to declare that the depth of prayer, contemplation and meditation should be taught, practiced and experienced with full honesty, clarity of mind and one-pointedness. A dying man's senses do not function properly. He gradually loses his eyesight, his tongue mumbles words which are not understood by others, and he is unable to express his thoughts through speech and actions. This painful and pitiable situation scares the mind in the case of non-meditators. But, if someone remembers the mantra for a long time in such a state of loneliness, the mantra starts leading him and this miserable period of loneliness and agony is over when mantra becomes his leader. Only one thought pattern is strengthened by remembering the mantra and it becomes predominant and leads the individual sufferer to his abode of peace, happiness and bliss. This experience has been validated by me personally after witnessing the death of many sages. I also witnessed the death of many rich men, scientists and so-called academicians and found them going through miserable agonies. Their facial expressions and helplessness were quite a proof for me that they did not prepare themselves for this last moment of life. I am not recommending any particular mantra coming from any particular source or tradition, but the magnanimity of mantra and meditation can be examined if you quietly observe a sage, a rich man or an intellectual when he is on his death bed.

Christians, Jews, Buddhists and Sufis all have their traditions, but a systematic meditation system has been lost in these great cultures. I don't even accept meditation as a part of any particular culture or religion, but as a scientific method and a prime necessity for everyone all over the world.

According to our lineage, there are two branches of teachers. One teaches the scriptures, observing austerities, and following the path of renunciation. The other branch is a branch of meditators and contemplators doing documentation experiments and scientifically collecting data on all levels of life, physical, energy level, level of sense perception and the way things are perceived on the mental level and finally on a spiritual level.

This book is a gift to the readers from our unbroken lineage of meditators to the students who are treading the inner path of light. For doing inner research, mantra and meditation are the greatest aids to the seekers. Let you not disturb your religion. But let you learn to know yourself on all levels. Let you also be aware of those fanatics who tell you not to meditate, for meditation is a condensed, deep and intense form of prayer which is not a man-centered prayer but is a God-centered prayer.

One who lives in the world can attain the highest state of *samadhi* through meditation. He is here, yet there. He lives in the world, yet above. He includes all and excludes none. Will there ever be a day when every man, woman and child begins practicing meditation? As a result, we can all attain the next step of civilization and realize the unity in life. Liberation can be attained here and now.

Dr. Pandit U. Arya has been faithfully following this path of meditation for many, many years. I am sure this book will help those who are on the path and those who are trying to be on the path.

Swami Rama
August 26, 1981

Part I

The Field of Mantra

1

Overview

The modern method of philosophical thought requires that the analyst look for a problem and then search for its solutions rather than merely stating a speculative hypothesis and presenting it as a solution to a problem that has not yet been stated. This latter method of thought was very well known to the ancient philosophers of India who systematized the yoga practices and their philosophical correlate, *Sankhya,* one of the most ancient formal systems of philosophy. The philosophers of the *Sankhya-yoga* system were most concerned with the problem of the pain of all living beings and not merely that of a given species, a particular individual or a specific time, place, situation or sequence. Their concern was not for specific pains and the means of finding pleasures to compensate for such pains but for the problem of pain itself. The subject of this book is not to state their entire philosophy concerning this issue but only to teach one of the methods whereby the pain of mind may be lessened. This method is meditation with a mantra.

The Lawbook of Manu states:

> All dependency on other than one's self is pain,
> Whatever is controlled by one's self is pleasure;

Know this to be, briefly, the definition
of pain and pleasure.

IV.160.

According to the Yoga Sutras of Patanjali, the Bible of
the yogis, the cause of pain is the ignorance of one's true nature,
and the means of the total eradication of pain is the rediscovery
of Self. Knowledge, in other words, is primarily defined as the
knowledge of the true nature of Self. All other knowledge
proceeds from this eternal wisdom. When the external knowledge of the world of objects is not directed and controlled from
this internal wisdom, that knowledge becomes destructive.

It is for this reason that humankind today is insecure as
to whether its formidable means of self-destruction will be
brought into use, thereby finally destroying whatever remains
of the fabric of society and of the sources of physical pleasure
and comfort that science has created for us. The yogi sees one
way out of this fear about humanity's possible self-destruction,
and that is to reawaken internalized knowlege. If one were to
ask the question, What would happen to all our scientific
discoveries and sources of physical comfort if the destructive
weapons of humankind were really wielded in an unwise
moment?, the yogi's answer would be that *ultimately* it may
have very little effect on the long-term future of human destiny.
After every dark age there is a golden age—this is the law of the
cycles of time. Human civilization and culture will recover itself
through the power and agency of knowledge, but the nature of
knowledge must be understood.

If dependency is pain, and knowledge alone is an
antidote to it, then dependency upon outer knowledge is self-
defeating and powerless to accomplish any purpose. In the long
run it will again lead to destruction. All knowledge is derived
from within. From where did the first man who invented the
wheel derive his knowledge of that wheel? If the word *wheel* was

proscribed from all the dictionaries of the world today, the pictures of all the wheels torn out, all the wooden wheels burnt and the iron ones melted down, a few centuries from now someone would yet envision a wheel and would certainly make one. Because the idea of a circle exists in the mind, in the wheels of the energy field, in the *chakras* in the *kundalini* stream, the mind observes these wheels within the subjective world. From there, it projects them into the objective world, shaping wood and metal to fashion the wheel after an internal image. The shapes and forms in the objective world are reminders of the energy fields and their force-patterns within ourselves, but when they are not treated as such, matter clashes with matter, and forms return to energy.

For this reason the ancient founding masters of yoga science engaged upon self-inquiry. If they were to appear to us as, in fact, they do, they would ask,

When you create a spaceship, the metal and machinery converted into the spaceship has made progress through the touch of human intelligence. When you can flash a light on or off, the light has made progress through the touch of your ingenuity. But what progress, human being, have *you* made in the past five thousand years? If you were left standing alone in a desert or a mountain cave without any material props, without anything external to depend on or project onto, if you stood absolutely naked in solitude and silence, what could you do with your six-foot frame? In what way are you an improvement on what the man five thousand years ago could do? Are your senses under greater control? Can you divert, through the application of your wisdom, the attention of an opponent from an attitude of conflict and turn his mind from war to peace? Can you control your anger today more than the man of five thousand years ago? Can

you pull yourself out of a depression without
paying another human fifty dollars an hour? Can
you slow down your breath and thus prolong your
life span? Can you improve your digestive function
internally, or permit greater absorption of life-
giving oxygen into your system? Can you, at will,
from within your body, produce antidotes to
poisons and pollutions administered to you by your
own product, civilization? And finally, can you
know and dwell in your ever-pure, ever-wise and
ever-free nature without being agitated by external
inducements?

These are the things that yogis can do. Their path leads to true
progress for humankind, but yours leads to the progress of
houses, ships, trains and other forms of metal and rock. These
are necessary for our physical comfort, but they are not
necessarily comforting for the mind, as the increasing incidence
of mental disturbance in modern civilization attests to.

A meditator's preoccupation is with the internal person,
not with the external tools of physical comfort. The modern
man changes his environment; the meditator changes his
person to fit the environment and to benefit from it. The
modern man changes the temperature of his room; the yogi
changes the temperature of his own body to fit that of the room.
All the great civilizations have left ancient monuments starting
from the pyramids, but in India no pyramids are to be found,
although the civilization is as old or older than that of Egypt.
Even the religious rituals performed at that time were around
altars constructed temporarily and then dismantled, imitating
the universal cycles of creation and dissolution. No altar,
religious sanctum or building was left after the ritual was
completed. The worship of the impermanent is a mark of
materialistic cultures that dwell mostly on the conception of the
immortality of the body or the preservation thereof. The yogi

seeks the permanent within—not the transient but the transcendental.

Many thousands of years ago—no one is certain of the exact date—when the pioneers of the culture and civilization of India were beginning to settle down, establishing villages and building cities in the valleys of the rivers Sindhu, Brahmaputra, Ganga (Ganges), Narmada, Krishna and Godavari, some wise beings withdrew from this development of civilization and established their ashrams,

> in the foothills and caves of the mountains,
> and the confluences of the rivers
> (where) one becomes wise through
> meditative wisdom.
>
> *Rig Veda VII.6.28*

They embarked on a journey of self-inquiry and self-discovery, looking into the highest possible potential of the physical body, the internal organs, senses, breath, all different levels of the mind, and finally reaching into the very core of spiritual energy. They developed a methodical system, charting out maps of consciousness and ways in which the relatively more inner sheaths of human faculties control and direct the forces in the progressively outer ones. Along the way, they discovered the means for improving and enjoying the health of all the faculties, beginning from the outermost skin of the body to the depth of the centralmost powers of the mind. They treated themselves as guinea pigs for the sake of internal experimentation on the mind.

During these experiments they induced states of consciousness in the mind and observed them at the same time. They also observed the effects of these alterations in mental states on their general psychological development as well as on their physical faculties and functions. Thousands of people came from the cities and the villages looking for peace and health in their ashrams. It was here that all the secular sciences such as astronomy and mathematics, as well as the political and social sciences were developed and taught—always within the context of spirituality and never outside of it. It was here that the masters trained their disciples through strict discipline into the ways and means of entering the inner secrets of the body, mind and consciousness. This master-disciple tradition still continues unbroken, and it is in this tradition that the mantras are handed down.

The modern science of psychology is also an experimental science, no doubt. Experimentation is based on observation of the behavior of others, human and nonhuman, and of chemical factors involved in the hormonal flow in the physical personality. This type of experimentation does not lead to any kind of self-cultivation on the part of the psychologist, however. Millions of dollars are used to make a million mice run through mazes, and one might presume that if there were two million mice, perhaps we would know twice as much about the mind! This is certainly not the case. Modern psychology studies the mind mainly in its disturbed or depressed states, whereas yoga psychology studies the mind in its calm and tranquil states. In other words, the emphasis in one is on illness and in the other on health.

No doubt, a large number of people experiment with their lives, and this may be considered a form of self-experimentation. But it is not in the same category as the self-experimentation conducted by the yogi. Self-experimentation today is mostly in pursuit of pleasures and exciting experiences; it is tied to the ephemeral objects of the world. It is not purely with the mind nor within the mind alone. This is the most important point of departure for the yogi because his experimentation is without any reference to external objects, but it is *with* the mind and *within* the mind alone. Modern man naturally induces mental states through his self-experimentations, but such self-experimentation is not methodical, because there is no understanding of the maps of consciousness on the part of the experimenter. According to the masters of the yoga tradition, only one who has established total control, *nirodha,* over all the mental faculties is qualified to, and capable of, making any efficacious experimentations. Otherwise, one will be lost in the mazes of the mind and end up confused, and perhaps pathologically disturbed.

This often occurs also in the case of the disciple who follows a master for a certain period, until the ego takes over and the disciple says, "I am qualified enough, capable enough, developed enough, to be self-dependent." He then moves off on his own, with half-baked powers and premature self-evaluation. Many such disciples have found themselves falling to destruction, but a great master never experiments haphazardly. He follows well-defined paths through the veils, mazes and chambers of the inner person and has a clear view of the goal that is enlightenment and self-realization. Without establishing such internal control, the mind can become disturbed or depressed and simply add more problems to itself than it is capable of solving. One of the very first internal controls is the mantra, with its methodical applications chosen according to the pathways being explored or the particular state of consciousness awaiting to be evoked.

For a person on the path of meditation, it is absolutely essential, as we have said above, to understand the principle of self-dependency. In other words, no props are permitted; no one can be blamed for one's own misfortunes or failures in matters of business or difficulties in emotional relationships. One is concerned entirely with improving oneself to such a degree that he can create heaven where there was hell in relationships. One is entirely responsible for one's own life's failures and successes and must not go about looking for posts, pillars and walls to lean against, with every person he meets.

When no such props are permitted for the mind, it will for a while look for replacements for these sources of support within the individual's own personality, and it is most likely that one will then become dependent on what the Buddha called *arupa-raga,* an attachment to the formless worlds within oneself. One may look for lights, sounds, celestial messages, imaginings, images, dreams, hallucinations, aspirations to astral travel, powers of prediction and prophecy, and many other such diversions and distractions. A truly aspiring initiate is permitted none of these, but he may resort to one single prop to replace them all: the mantra. One may form no intellectual or emotional assocations with this, but simply maintains a neutral relationship with the presence that makes itself felt like a magnet that magnetizes a piece of iron, without any effort on the part of either. When one has learned to absorb the mantra into the subconscious mind, gradually many other problems arising in meditation simply evaporate.

Imagine a cave explorer who enters the cave and passes through many narrow passages, twisting paths, wider halls, and finally arrives at the end of the cave at a huge hall where he finds a vast treasure. On the way back he unravels a ball of thread all along the way, and when he comes out he hands the other end of the thread to a friend, saying, "If you simply follow this thread into the cave and keep following it through many passageways, you will arrive at the end in a hall filled with a huge treasure." The friend is dubious and cynical, but the promise of a treasure prompts him. He looks in, but he is afraid of the dark and looks out again. The promise of the treasure is repeated, so he enters and goes a few steps but then goes out again. Gradually, he gathers courage to go deeper and deeper, and finally one day he also arrives at the shining precious treasure.

The ancient masters, and those who continue their tradition today, have thus explored the passageways that lead one to the riches hidden within all of us. The mantra and the accompanying concentration on breath is that thread which is handed to the student when a qualified teacher imparts a mantra. At this point the mantra is simply a few words or sounds, but if the charted map of consciousness is followed under the direction of an experienced teacher, it will finally lead, through many states of mental awareness, to the deepest possible silence where dwells the knowledge of eternity. Indeed, the knowledge of mantras was so treasured that its secrets were unveiled only to one's dearest and most deserving students.

We are reminded of the story of Manu, the great lawgiver, whose youngest son was away studying at an ashram. Manu decided to distribute his entire wealth to his children, and gave away all his material possessions. Many years later when the young boy returned as a graduate, he asked his father, "You have given away all of your wealth to my brothers; why did you not save anything for me?" Manu replied, "I have saved for you the most precious of my possessions: thirty-eight mantras that were revealed through me. These I will teach you."

In the *Rig Veda,* the ancientmost collection of twenty thousand mantras, these thirty-eight occur in Book X, *suktas* 61 (27 mantras) and 62 (11 mantras). Their authorship is attributed to Nabhanedishtha, the son of Manu. In the beginning of the recitation of the mantras, the authorship of the ancient *rishis* is recited as an act of gratitude. We have used the word authorship here for the want of a better word, but later we shall explain what exactly is meant by the process of revelation leading to such authorship.

In the following chapters, we attempt an explanation of the origin of mantras, the psychological and linguistic theories pertaining to the mantra science, as well as guidelines for the practice of mantra in meditation. It should, however, be borne in mind that the book is merely an outline, a map. It is not the country itself, which must be traveled in the company of an expert guide.

2

A Family of Words

It is well known that the languages of Europe are united with those of India, the homeland of the yogis, in the single Indo-European language family. When Western scholars traveling east in the wake of the European conquests rediscovered Sanskrit in India during the 18th and 19th centuries, they held the view that Sanskrit was the mother of all the European languages. Gradually, this view changed, and the present opinion of Western scholars is that it is the seniormost surviving language of the Indo-European language family and the senior sister of Latin and ancient Greek. It is well recognized that many words in the English language are directly or indirectly derived from Sanskrit, the same language in which the literature of the yoga tradition is passed on orally as well as textually.

Below we quote from the Living Webster Dictionary of the English Language, the 1975 edition, about the origin of the words *man* and *mind:*

> Man, man, *n.* pl. men [O.E. *man, mann,* man, person=D., O.H.G., and Sw. *man,* G. *mann,* Icel, *mathr, mannr,* Dan. *mand,* Goth. *Manna* < root

man, to think, seen in Skt. *man,* to think, *manas,* mind, *manushya,* man.] A human being ......

Mind, mind, *n.* [O.E. *mynd, gemnyd,* mind, thought, intention; Dan. *minde,* Icel. *minni,* memory; < root *man,* to think, seen also in *mean,* to intend; L. *mens, mentis,* mind (whence *mental*); Gr. *menos,* mind.]

Briefly, the English words *man, mind,* and *mental,* from Latin *mens* as well as Greek *menos,* are all derived from the Sanskrit verb root *man* meaning to think, to contemplate, to meditate. Take for example, *Nomen Actionis* from the verb root *man.* The word *manana* is translated by V.S. Apte's Sanskrit English Dictionary, one of the most authentic, as *thinking, reflection, meditation, cogitation.* The Webster dictionary, however, has indicated the verb *man* to mean only *think.* This type of mistake is often made by Western linguists and other scholars because they do not understand the multilevel nature of the meaning of Sanskrit words. The verb root *man* signifies any mentation, but this cannot be understood without comprehending the nature and functions of mind. The yogis regard mind to be a multilevel entity, a force-field constituted of layers upon layers of energy, and at each level its function differs and its faculties are diverse.

As an aspiring inquirer into the nature of self proceeds deeper and deeper to unravel the mysteries of the mind, he finds that beyond the random thought processes, there is a faculty which serves as an instrument of contemplation and thereafter leads to meditation. Our purpose here is not to discuss the nature of mind, however, but simply to understand the verb root *man* so that we may understand the English words *man* and *mind.* Whatever qualities and actions may be signified by its verb root, *mind* is the substratum or locus of those, and *man* is the possessor and user of mind in its totality.

Even though the thinking process alone is sufficient to separate human beings from the rest of living creation, we must bear in mind the human capacity to continue to evolve mentally. The physical evolution of the various species may or may not have occurred at the level of the gross body, but when we arrive at the human species, development and evolution are mental and spiritual. The English word *man* and its counterparts in other Indo-European languages encompass and include not merely the capacity for thought but also the realization of the highest potential which is experienced in the state of *samadhi,* the ultimate meditation. The word *man* connotes all of it, the entire journey from thought to the transcendence beyond mind, for mind remains a useful instrument only up to the cognitive stage of transcendence, *samprajnata samadhi.* In the ultimate *samadhi,* the *asamprajnata,* the yogi has no further use even for the mental processes because he dwells in the nature of the spiritual self which is beyond even the entire energy-field of the mind. Yet, so long as he maintains the physical appearance of a human being he is called a man, a being who has evolved from a thinker into the indweller of this ever pure, ever wise, ever free, transcendental spiritual nature.

The word *mantra* is also derived from the same verb root *man.* For a meditator, mantra is the object of thought, contemplation and meditation, progressively. In the first stages, an initiate merely repeats the mantra thought, then learns to remember it. When so advised by the meditation teacher, he may contemplate what it signifies and to what experience it leads. Finally, it permeates the entire mind. Having replaced random thoughts at the thinking stage and intellectual processes at the contemplative stage, the mantra finally purifies the subconscious impulses and emotions and becomes the thread leading from the finite transient to the infinite transcendental. To understand the relationship of the triad man, mind and mantra is to understand the entire process of meditation. We

shall discuss this process later in this work.
From the same verb root *man* is derived the word *muni*,
a contemplative, meditative hermit, or a monk. Dictionaries
suggest that the derivation of the word *monk* is the Greek
monos, meaning one, single, or alone, but I suspect the word
has some relationship with the word *muni.* As the thinking man
becomes contemplative and the contemplative becomes meditative, so the meditative, having absorbed the mind into the
mantra, the object of meditation becomes a *muni,* the highest
epitome of the spiritual evolution of man. The ancient *muni*
hymn in the *Rig Veda* states:

> Drunk by what proceeds by silence
> we flourish on the airs, *pranas;*
> You mortals merely see
> our physical bodies.
>
> *X.136.3*

The seven *rishis,* the seers of the seven mantras of this hymn, are
called *vata-rashanah,* they who hold the reins of the wind,
meaning the *pranas.* The attribute of a *muni* is the practice of
mauna, the common word used for silence. One silences the
random thought process, intellectual pursuits and even contem-
plations of mysteries as the mind centers on the mantra, and
finally the mantra becomes a vibration and merges into the
deepest inner silence of *samadhi.* This silence is no mere absence
of words, but it is the mother of all creativity.
To explain this idea of creativity, we would like to refer
to the legend of Manu, who is regarded as the first human
being, the first king, the first lawgiver of mankind. The Sanskrit
word for human is *manushya,* the offspring of Manu. The
name of Manu is associated with the Indian story of the great
flood(s). It is thought that the cycles of creation and dissolution
are divided into fourteen periods known as *manv-antaras,* that

is, Manu-intervals. It is always a Manu who leads a living creation, especially human beings, across the primordial floods. Let us pay attention here to the story of Noah whose original name in Hebrew and Arabic is *Nuh*. The Sanskrit form of Manu in the nominative singular is also *Manuh*. It would appear that the initial sound of M has been dropped and the *Manuh* and *Nuh* are identical. We leave this thought for the students of comparative religion.

In the Indian tradition, there are fourteen floods in a single cycle of creation and dissolution—seven in the ascendant part of the cycle and seven again in the descendant part. Specific names are assigned to these Manu-intervals in the texts on astronomy. As is the case with a great many myths, legends and even stories that appear in the ancient texts from the Vedas to the Bible, it seems that this particular flood motif simply represents the movement of energy flooding upwards through the seven centers of consciousness to the divine principle, as well as energy flowing downwards from the divine into the human. The meaning of the word *Manu* becomes clearer when we read the texts on the science of mantra in which the word *mantra* is used less often but the word Manu is used as a synonym for mantras. The creative principle of the mantras, when personified, becomes Manu. The silence of this creative being brings forth all the laws for human society, and Manu is thus regarded as the first lawgiver and author of *Manu-smrti*, the Book of Laws.

Here we relate the Indian story of the flood:

> One morning when the great Manu went to the river flowing through his ashram for his morning ablutions, he saw a little fish that had entered his water vessel. He was about to throw the little fish back into the river when the fish beseeched him, "Do not throw me out, Manu. Nurture me and I shall be helpful to you." Manu kept the fish in the

vessel, but it grew too large, so he let it go into the ashram pond. Soon the pond was too small for the fish, and the fish asked to be taken to the river again. Before the fish said farewell, he told Manu that soon there would be a great flood covering all of the earth, that he should build a huge ark, and that when he had built it, he should remember the fish, who would then come to Manu. Within a few days the flood waters began to rise, so Manu completed the work of building the ark and remembered the fish, which was none other but the Lord incarnate. The fish had sprouted a single horn (origin of the unicorn?) and asked Manu to tie the rope to the horn. The fish led the boat over the waters for a long time until finally the waters began to recede. Then the fish brought the boat to a mountain peak of the Himalayas called *Naukaban-dhana,* advised Manu to disembark and commanded him to undergo a great deal of *tapas,* ascetic observances, whereby he would be able to start again the cycle of the procreation of the species.

There are many versions of the story, including those describing the manifestation of the female principles to mate with Manu and those describing his reentry finally into a meditative mode to bring forth laws by which human beings may abide. It is interesting to note that the fish is the symbol of the second center of consciousness. This center also represents the principle of cosmic waters. It is here in *svadhishthana* that the *kundalini* force dwells, constituting the entire creative energy of the universe and of the human personality, and from here it is raised to the higher centers until it bursts forth at the peak of the crown. All of this—the ascendance and return of the flood waters of energy to bring forth the laws of control to the lower centers—cannot occur without the proper use of a mantra, the Manu principle itself. It is by this process of the awakening of the innermost spiritual power that man first becomes the *muni* and the *muni* then becomes a Manu, the law-giver, the very embodiment of the creative principle.

At one time, the traditions of yoga so permeated the society of India that even in social-political principles, the spiritual laws were applied at every step. For example, a person who has a mantra is called a *mantrin* or *mantri*. This is the word used throughout for a king's minister, and even in the present secular democratic state of India, the secretary of any organization is called a *mantri*. Even the Prime Minister of India is called *pradhana-mantri,* the chief mantra-keeper!

We have gone into detail regarding the words related to mantra to show that the principle underlying the initiation and practice of mantra transcends all cultural barriers, all national boundaries and all linguistic differences. When Western society rediscovers its origins in the spiritual traditions of the East, it will enhance its cultural richness in the same way as the acceptance of the Indian numerals between the thirteenth and fifteenth centuries helped develop the science of mathematics in Europe. It is only through a proper exchange between the sciences of the East and the West that humanity will discover its common inheritance.

3

The Sounds and the Psyche

We have explained that the word *human* is derived from the Sanskrit word *manushya,* meaning the child of Manu, which is the personification of the principle of mantra. In other words, the practice of meditation takes the raw material—a mere thinking human being—and refines him into a *manushya,* a child of his own mantra. If the initiate cultivates his mantra, the mantra cultivates him, creates for him a mental culture from which all of his external culture flows. In this way, the creativity of *manu* manifests itself again and again through the human mind. The mind that has learned to concentrate on a single object generates a new high voltage of power so that the personality owning such a mind does not easily waver, abandon, quit or move away from situations of conflict or from difficult undertakings. The problems that loomed large before, though maintaining the same size objectively, now shrink to minute proportions subjectively. One takes on more and more responsibilities until finally one takes the vow of a *bodhi-sattva:* "I shall not hesitate; I shall not step back; I shall not enter final liberation until every living being from a blade of grass to the entire soul of the universe has been enlightened and liberated from the cycles of ignorance and pain." Such a person is no longer a person but the very moving spirit behind all the cultural developments of humankind. He truly becomes a lawgiver. The words spoken by such masters have reverberated around this planet for thousands of years and will continue to do so.

The mantra is like a planted seed waiting to be cultivated, nurtured and cultured. We shall describe the ways of nurturing and culturing the mantra later. The mantra, thus cultivated, cultures the mind, purifies it, refines it and makes its perceptions sharp and concentrated. A person with a mind so cultivated is capable of reaching the utmost possible heights in any art, science, social pursuit or pinnacle of power. But he has taken the vow of embarking on a one-pointed journey, the end of which is seldom in sight—he wishes to remove the pain of *all* those who are in suffering. If the readers who have been practicing their mantra for a few months or years feel that nothing so dramatic has happened to them, then let them understand that they have not yet begun to cultivate their mantra nor have they allowed the mantra to culture the mind through the incessant practice of mindfulness twenty-four hours of a day. If they were truly to cultivate themselves, the presence of the mantra would be felt at all times—even before one awoke from sleep, one would be aware of the presence of the mantra. In the case of an accident, there would not be the sound of "Aw!" or "Oh!" emerging from the mouth, but simply the mantra would come out as the loudest sound in the mind. Even in the arms of one's lover, one would enjoy the presence of mantra imparting the power of concentration on the pleasure at hand, yet with a certain restraint, a certain neutrality about it, granting control over one's self and over the best means of developing the given experience in an expert manner.

How is it possible that a simple sound or word can have

such power to culture a human being? It is here that we must embark on an elucidation of the principles of psycholinguistics that underlie the theory and practice of mantra. The relationship of mind and language is studied by modern linguists in great depth, and the psychological effects of language are known in some detail. However, in talking of mantras we are not talking of language. Most initiates of many years' standing in their practice still use their mantra under the conception that these are words of a non-English foreign language, the meaning of which is unintelligible to them. This we shall discuss later, but here it is essential to point out that each sound unit, syllable or phoneme, is regarded in the Tradition as *akshara,* an eternal vibration that dwells in the knowledge of the Superconscious. When uttered, it vanishes from the audibility scale, but as knowledge, it never disappears; it is never lost. This idea is akin to the theory in physics relating to the conservation of energy. No fresh form of energy can ever be created nor can it ever be destroyed. On this fundamental principle the teachers of Sanskrit linguistics called the letters *aksharas,* literally "the undestroyables," "immutables" or "imperishables."

In a later section of this work, we shall explain the origins of the mind energy that receives the thought vibration of syllables, responds to them and refines them, but here, suffice it to say that the arising of a syllable in the form of a thought, which we shall refer to from now on as a syllabic thought unit, constitutes in the mind a merger of two different types of energies creating subtle vibrations. Very early in the history of the yoga tradition, as well as in Sanskrit linguistics, it was recognized that each syllable of the alphabet is attuned to particular powers, faculties and attributes of the mind. In other words, different syllables have different effects on the mental energy. The syllabic quanta may thus be easily called psychic quanta. The human mind thinks in terms of either visual images—that is, patterns of light, or in words—that is, units of sound. We have said earlier that whatever thoughts arise in the mind they immediately become inputs as the memory of such thought arousal is stored in the deep recesses of the personality.

The basic unit of thought is the word and that of the word is the syllable. However, it needs to be emphasized again and again that here we are not talking simply of the effect of language on psychology and the way the human psyche produces language communication, but rather of the very fact of the syllabic thought production having an impact on the overall development of the mind. Take for instance, a complete stranger who has never heard English spoken. Approach him in a strange country and say, "Thud!" He would immediately realize that something violent and inimical has been done to him. The kind of impression the sound carries conveys an intent, an impression of certain force and power on to his mind, and his response will not be very friendly. Then select another person to whom you say softly, "Lull!" The impression conveyed to him by this sound is entirely opposite to 'thud', even though this latter person has also never heard the English language spoken. This ability of sounds without translated meaning to convey an impression on the mind is not limited to onomatopoeic words, but such words are merely the gross examples of the similar capacity of all sounds to produce mental effect.

Let us look at it from a slightly different angle. Your personality is constituted of the sum total of all the thoughts you have ever had. By personality we mean the total mental content because it is the mind's content that is reflected in the body position, gesture and attitude. All one's choices and inclinations are the product of the totality of the chemistry of thoughts. It is not a single immediate thought that is producing a gesture of your eyebrow, but behind that one gesture lies the accumulation of many lifetimes. Every act that one performs, every word one speaks, every flicker of light or color one perceives even unconsciously, subliminally, from the corner of his eye, and every thought that has ever arisen in the form of rational argument or feeling, emotion, memory, hallucination, fantasy or dream are all stored in the memory banks of the mind, in a corner of what the yogis call *chitta.*

The yogis believe that a person is capable of cultivating a certain type of personality by choice and design. It is not merely a desirable trait but the right way of life based on a sound philosophy, that everything in a human being should be directed by his power of free volition and not as a by-product of helpless habits and dependencies or simple momentums arising from the subconscious. The reading of this book is not an act forced on the reader; rather, it is being done of one's own volition. Thousands of lifetimes (or if one doesn't believe in reincarnation, millions of uncountable moments of experience) have finally produced this momentum, driving one to read through these passages. If read by free choice and with total conscious observation, then it leads to freedom.

As you read these passages, you are at this very moment cultivating certain qualities in your mental personality as the imprint of these thoughts is left on you. Even if this imprint is very minute in comparison to all the other similar *samskaras* that have been accumulated from before, its positive power is bound to be of some result, if not as an independent thought process or volitional direction, then by its influence on the total chemistry of the mind.

Furthermore, whatever would be repeatedly introduced in the mind will become the mind's habit. A certain thought arises; it triggers the memories of some pleasant associations and the thinker pursues it, thereby strengthening its force, inviting it to return to the mind at another opportune moment. One day you

spread out your lounge chair under the warm

summer sun, stretch out your body, close your eyes
in the warmth and say to yourself, "Now, what shall
I fantasize about today!" You allow your mind free
rein to bring forth all kinds of relevant or irrelevant
associations and savor their presence. Someone
rings the doorbell; the fantasy is broken but you
enjoyed it. Another day you take up where you left
off.

In this way one keeps giving a certain force, a power, to
certain types of thoughts until the thought, repeated often
enough, becomes a desire. A simple desire becomes a craving;
the unfulfilled craving leads to frustration; the craving and
frustration together, as the *Bhagavad Gita* says *(II.62-64),* leads
to a confusion of mind. This confusion brings an absence of
self-awareness, a loss of the freedom of volition, and a helpless
habit develops. The same thought, same desire, same craving,
same frustration, same confusion recurs again and again,
becoming a fixation, a compulsion, an unconscious personality
trait.

In this way our *karma,* the collective series of this type of
mental action, creates in our person an attraction towards
certain objects and situations. Each object or situation, however, carries its own unpleasant side effects, for there is always
some kind of a pain prevalent, either in the cause or in the
continuity or in the effect, of even a pleasant situation. Very
soon we begin to curse our situation, thinking that we have been
brought into it unfairly, not knowing that it was only our
unconscious personality traits, cultivated by our own choice of
repeated sequences of thought over a period of time, that had
made of us the kind of magnets that would attract and draw a
certain type of situation, surroundings, association and accompaniment to us.

A meditator realizes the power he has over the development of his own personality. He gives it a reality simply by

applying his choice of will, which is more powerful than all of the previous thought habits, cravings, frustrations, confusions, fixations, compulsions, personality traits and consequent situations. He knows that the true agent of action is the reflection of *purusha,* the universal Conscious Principle, falling in the mirror of the inward face of *buddhi,* the faculty of intuitive discrimination, the finest of the faculties of mind—which in itself is the quintessence of all the essences of nature. Yes, mind is the quintessence of all the essences of nature, but the Consciousness Principle in us has mastery over it. Thus its controlling power, through this quintessence, extends over the very essences of all nature. With such controlling power residing in our conscious volition, how can we ever be in any kind of a helpless situation?

Those who blame their circumstances or associations for their misfortunes, whether in their past or in the present, whether in personal or in business relationships, simply do not realize that the causes of their difficulties are in the fact that their own minds are confused and disorganized. Meditation is the process of having the mind again clarified and reorganized. It is putting the house of one's internal personality into order. This reordering of the internal personality begins with the practice of a single thought, the mantra, which serves as a "drop of the golden sun" into the darkness that previously prevailed. It is like a culture to convert milk into yogurt—a tiny amount will do and will soon cover the entire contents of the vessel.

We have now stated clearly that a thought repeated often enough becomes a natural habit. Furthermore, syllables as thought units are not mere processes of the conscious mind, like those of ordinary language that can be translated. They carry with themselves the capacity to serve as a culture, a spore, a seed, so that a little bit suffices to eventually fill a large space and to convert it into its own likeness.

Suppose a person were to hear the sound "thud" involuntarily. Suppose now that he were to hear the sound voluntarily each day. Even if he has not yet discovered that it is a word from the English dictionary, will not the sound carry an impression on his mind? What will be the final constitution of his personality after he has completed this practice of listening to the sound? Now imagine if someone were to repeat the sound "lull" similarly, a half hour a day for some months or years to come. In what way will the constitution of his mental personality be altered? What new psychological traits will develop in him? In what way will it alter his choices, behavior patterns and finally the situations, associations and the company to which he is drawn and that is drawn to him? How will it affect the relationships he will enter into and the way in which he will interpret those relationships, in turn, reabsorbing all of these impressions again into his mind's chemistry to cultivate fresh momentum towards new choices?

What we have described here is the process of *karma*—the entire interaction of mental, vocal and physical deeds, their results, and through the reabsorption of these results, a reaction, a fresh action again from the mind, speech and body. This vicious circle will continue until a factor from outside of it is introduced to alter the pattern. The mantra is a thought which is neither originated from nor is itself the origin of this type of helpless pattern; rather, it is that extra factor which draws to itself the energy that is ordinarily going into helpless, disorderly personality patterns. The mantra reshapes that energy and returns it to the faculties of the mind in a freshly created order, in place of the prevailing chaos.

The ancient masters who treated themselves as guinea pigs in order to develop the science of self-discovery, tried out all the various sound patterns and carefully recorded the impact that the practice of such meditative thought left on the very subtle recesses of their mental personalities. They may not have studied the words *thud* or *lull,* but rather they tried the syllables whose many possible combinations and permutations would leave the most positive, desirable effects on the mind. These effects will be two-fold:

> 1) clearing away the undesirable tendencies of the mind, and
> 2) cultivating the desirable tendencies of the mind.

In other words, this means:

> 1) healing the mental illnesses and filling the weak spots, and
> 2) bringing strength to the most positive powers within the mind.

The reader must have inferred from our argument by now that various combinations of syllables must be matched to the needs of different personalities. A person comes asking wise counsel of a master or of his qualified disciple, complaining of certain weaknesses in his mind and consequently in his life and relationships. The yogi, having perceived the inner workings of the mind, states, "You lack a certain fire in your mind and personality. I shall give you a fire mantra." The seeker is given a combination of syllables scientifically appropriate to his needs and is advised to recite or mentally repeat, or better still, to remember it intensively for, say, a half hour every day, and generally throughout his wakeful day as well. He may even be advised to gaze at a certain flame or to visualize a similar flame within one of the centers of consciousness while practicing the remembrance of the mantra. The teacher may advise the initiate to practice the mantra with even-flowing breath and to repeat it once with each breath, or he may suggest a greater frequency. On the other hand, he might advise using the mantra without awareness of the breath, or with concentration on one particular center of consciousness, or simply advise one to keep the mantra in the mind in whatever way it arises naturally.

There are many different ways of practicing the mantra so that the psychic content of the syllable has the optimum effect on the mind and so that it generates the type of power desired according to one's weaknesses and strengths, according to the path of meditation that the teacher considers most appropriate for the *sadhaka* (student). Another person suffering from worldly disturbances may also seek similar counsel, and this person may be advised to practice a water mantra.

Terms such as *fire mantra, water mantra, solar mantra* and *lunar mantra* are very common in the texts, as well as in the oral and initiatory traditions in which the mantras are imparted. These terms indicate the particular power of the certain syllabic combinations, but of these we shall speak later in some detail. Let us again reiterate the psychological principle behind the mantra.

When someone finds himself helpless with anger, this author often advises him to sit by flowing waters and simply observe the flow. It is not possible for one to really observe the flow of cooling water and the peace of its surroundings without calming his anger. If someone suffers from depression, we advise him to watch the flames of a blazing fire for if one continues to watch these flames the depression must lift. If it is true that an emotion can be altered in this way simply by introducing the effect of a natural phenomenon, then how much more impressive will the results be if one were to perform similar observations, chosen according to one's psychological need and under expert guidance, repeatedly, over a period of time, or if one simply visualized the memory of such a natural phenomenon?

We have said earlier that the mind is the quintessence of the essences of all nature. By observing a flaming fire or flowing water, one is not observing merely an external phenomenon but is awakening the latent quintessential power that exists in the mind. Natural phenomena may or may not have their own independent objective existence—different philosophers disagree on this point, and our purpose here is not to solve this particular problem—but according to the yoga system of psychology, objects are definitely interpreted by, or even projected from the relevant quintessential power resident in the mind. And each of these quintessential powers has its own specific *akshara-bija,* or syllabic seed.

4

Mantra as a Central Thought

We have not yet clarified the exact relationship between the mind, the natural phenomena, the powers of the specific seeds and the mode of their interaction. This we'll leave for later while we explore the mantra as a central thought.

The entire human life is comparable to a single sentence. It is a series of unbroken parts that begin when three beings unite and conception takes place. The combined particle of the mind of the parents is infused into the mind of the third being who has come to take abode in the world through their bodies. A rudimentary consciousness exists from the very moment of conception, and it continues to develop slowly. Many types of awareness and memories are added to this sentence, and this unbroken continuous thought process unfolds into a complexity unmatched in any other living being. Many strands of thought weave and interweave, creating the complex web of human personality. As the living days of the person begin to draw to an end, the web seems to unravel and finally the thought process becomes simpler and simpler. At the end only a single strand remains, which also trails off and vanishes. We have spoken of this process in greater detail in *Meditation and the*

Art of Dying.[1] There are no breaks in this continuous thought process, not even in sleep.

Many think that sleep is a state of unconsciousness, but that is not the case. Sleep is simply another type of thought—the thought of negation. It is only a thought fixed on the principle of universal negation. But below the shallow surfaces of the mind that wake and sleep, the rest of the mind continues its functions and duties. If the entire mind were to sleep, who would digest the food during the night and who would keep the lungs functioning? Who is it that hears the sound of the name being called when a person is asleep and decides to wake up? If the entire mind is asleep, who is it that turns a sleeping person on his side? Who is it that rolls to the edge of the bed and then warns the body not to fall off but turn back under the cover of the blanket? It is therefore obvious that the deeper mind never sleeps, and it is there that the meditative yogis often go to rest, still observing the surfaces of the mind. In the case of a deep meditator, the practice of mantra continues at that level even when these sleeping surfaces of the mind maintain a dormant consciousness.

Let us turn back, however, to the single sentence that is our life experience. If you really want to test whether this sentence of life is an unbroken continuity, observe the thought or the mood with which you go to sleep at night. Often you have dreams that are suggestive of the same mood and thought. But even if these dreams have not been vivid enough to remember, you will find that in the morning you pick up that very thought or mood and continue it into the rest of the day. Thus if you want to have a good morning upon waking tomorrow, then have a good night tonight. That is, go to sleep with a peaceful, gentle, contemplative thought, such as the relaxed practice of the mantra.

[1] Arya, Pandit U., *Meditation and the Art of Dying.* Honesdale, Pa: Himalayan Institute, 1979

The analogy of the life process as an unbroken continuous sentence is further useful in our understanding of the practice of mantra. Imagine that you are writing a letter to someone while in an angry and disturbed mood. The letter is filled with that type of emotion. While you are in the middle of writing a paragraph, the mailman brings your mail, and upon reading one particular letter, your mood changes. You do not wish to throw away the letter you were writing in the ugly mood, so instead of continuing your paragraph with an *and,* you add a *but* or an *if.* Immediately the entire theme of the letter changes and becomes expressive of a very positive mood.

It is thus that in the continuity of the strands of the complex paragraph of life, which is filled with many clauses, phrases and idioms, you add at this particular point in your life sentence (*karmic* pun intended!) a single syllable or a series of syllables called the mantra. However, unlike the *if* or the *but* in the paragraph of your letter, the mantra syllables are neutral. Yet by their mere neutrality they bring about a psychic effectiveness. They bring a new direction to one's life. They work on one at a subsurface level—the level at which the sleeping person does not sleep and the waking person remains simply a witness to the processes going on at the surface. Gradually the entire mood, the mode, and the pattern of life will undergo a change.

This change does not occur dramatically overnight, although some people expect that through receiving a mantra they will experience some dynamic, dramatic, immediate change. Someone once called me on the phone and said, "Dr. Arya, I received my mantra three months ago; when do I get my enlightenment?"

There may be special times, nonetheless, when dramatic changes do take place. I recall the incident of a particular person in a high profession who was very distressed and had attempted suicide several times. He was referred to Swami

Rama, who then asked me to give the person a mantra. After he received the mantra, he would often visit the Center for Higher Consciousness in an extremely agitated state and would say, "I am angry, I am terribly angry, I am dreadfully angry. I am angry all the time. I am angry at work; I am angry with my secretaries and with my colleagues. I am angry with myself. What have you done to me? Why am I so angry since I have received this mantra?"

Six months later when Swami Rama came to Minneapolis, the gentleman went to him, complaining, "Swamiji, do you know what your students are doing with people here? Ever since Dr. Arya gave me my mantra, I have been dreadfully angry, all the time. What has he done to me?"

Swamiji, in his usual patience, asked the gentleman, "And before you received your mantra, how were you feeling then?"

The person thought for a moment and said, "I was very depressed."

"Are you depressed now?" asked Swamiji.

The reply was "No, I'm not. I'm certainly not depressed, but I'm terribly angry!"

Swamiji said, "Do you realize that depression is simply suppressed anger, and your suppressed anger needed to be brought out to the surface?" Then he advised me to give the gentleman a mantra that would bring forth a state of equilibrium, assimilating that energy which was going into anger.

It is thus that yogis often lead their students to various states and moods, though the students may not understand, at the time, that the change occurs through the initiator's intervention.

However, not everyone who receives a mantra should expect changes as dramatic as the one in the above example. Changes in the human personality occur very slowly and imperceptibly. Look at your face in a mirror tonight, have a good sleep, wake up tomorrow morning, and see that face in the mirror again. Has it changed? Not a bit. Again look at it this evening and tomorrow morning, and continue in this way to look at your face twice daily. Does it change from the morning to the evening or from the evening to the morning? No. But, five years from now, compare the photograph taken of you today with your face in the mirror. Which night did you go to sleep and wake up with a changed face? The change was taking place continuously, but it was not perceived by you as you were undergoing the change. This directly applies to the life of a meditator. The changes that will occur through the mantra will be imperceptible, but over a period of time, they will become manifest.

Here let us deal with another question that many practitioners of meditation ask their teachers. They say, "I was having good meditations, but I do not know what has happened lately. I do not want to sit, or I am distracted in meditation. In one morning's meditation I was transported to a state of great tranquility, but since then, nothing; I draw a blank."

Others who have meditated for longer periods report similar interchanging cycles of ups and downs in the experience of meditation. What is the cause of such changes? Sometimes the input from daily life disturbs one and causes the mind to become unsettled. But yogis speak of an entirely different level of existence in human experience. This is called the world of *samskaras,* and the commentaries of the Yoga Sutras of Patanjali have gone into this in great detail. The *samskaras* are the imprints left on the subtle body and the *chitta* (the totality of the mind stuff) over many, many incarnations. The individual *samskaras* await the introduction of fresh *samskaras,* each of their own likeness, so that they can gather force. When certain types of *samskaras* have gathered sufficient force, they have the capacity to alter the effects of the sum total of all *samskaras,* thus determining

> The kind of species in which one would be born,
> the life span in the particular body, and
> the types and intensities of pains and
> pleasures during that life span.

This is called the process of *karma,* but another area on which the *samskaras* have a strong influence is in developing our inclinations. The *samskaras* begin to procure and produce *vasanas,* other potentialities, which then become realities in the whole of conscious inclinations and choices. It is through these conscious inclinations and choices that we determine the nature of our life situation, what we add to our relationships, and how we interpret what we derive from them in return.

The world of *samskaras* is not a dormant, sleeping, inert world. It is very active in the unconscious mind. By the word *unconscious* we do not mean that the mind itself is unconscious. Please understand this carefully. I repeat that by the word *unconscious* it is not meant that the mind itself is unconscious. But the surface part of the mind that is primarily conscious of the external objective phenomena is not conscious of what is going on in the so-called unconscious mind. It is only from the relative point of view of the surface consciousness that the word *unconscious* is used.

The yogi, as a true witness to all the processes going on within him, is not unconscious of the world of *samskaras.* But to the average person, who has chosen to ignore the inner witness within himself, the processes going on in the world of *samskaras* might seem as nothing, as if all the past imprints are lying inert, doing nothing. The fact, however, is that there is a dynamic movement going on at that level. In the Yoga Sutras it is called the *parinama,* the constant change or alteration. This is very much like the dynamic ocean flow of undertows, currents, tides and huge sub-oceanic rivers of force that are not visible from the surface. An amateur observer, knowing nothing of oceanography, knows only of the surface waves, the ebb and wash of the tide on the beach. But that is not the view of the expert.

It is the world of *samskaras* that truly creates the currents and cross-currents of our lives. Swami Rama has said that six months before anything is to happen in the gross world of ordinary phenomena of which we are conscious, something first happens in the subtle world of which an ordinary person is not aware. So, even though there may be no effect in one's life outwardly, something which develops in the world of *samskaras* brings forth subtle forces to the surface of the mind, because of which it feels calmer than usual or more disturbed than before, deeper or shallower in meditation, suddenly drawn towards or unreasonably averse to certain colors or types of interactions.

This type of unpredictable change occurring in moods of the mind and modes of one's life situations puzzles the young initiate. But the yogi learns to dive deeply into the world of hidden *samskaras* and often gives them a nudge in the direction he chooses for his life or even, compassionately, for a better life for his students. By entering into the subsurface levels of the universal *chitta,* the mind-field, the yogi is able to see the direction of its flow. When a master imparts the mantra, it is with this direction in mind that he intuitively imparts the mantra most effective for the benefit of the student.

In other words, a mantra may be regarded as an antidote to the *karmic* process. We have understood by now that our *karma* is constituted of all the impressions that are left on the mind from our past words and actions, from outputs, and from inputs *from within and without.* In all the texts, such as the *Bhagavad Gita,* that deal with the *karmic* process, and also in the teachings of all great yogis, we are advised to neutralize our *karma.* This is to be done by performing our acts without seeking the benefits, by being conscientious about their perfection for their own sake and for the benefit of others while seeking no fruits for ourselves, and being alike in victory and defeat—not laughing in gains nor crying in losses.

It is difficult, however, for an average person to lead such a life all the time. But through the practice of mantra and meditation, one can add a dimension to life which is absolutely neutral with regard to all the external losses and gains. The *karmic* effectiveness of the mantra will then work in several different ways at several different levels simultaneously. One maintains the mantra practice with a sense of neutrality, yet with complete inward absorption, even while carrying on one's daily work and remaining uninvolved with daily emotions.

While the *chitta,* the substratum of the storage of our *karma,* is receiving the *samskaras* of our involvements, it is also at the same time receiving the imprint of the neutral observance of our mantra. In this way, the internal impact of the power of our emotional involvement is greatly reduced. The great ups and downs of internal life are made even. The *samskaras* of attractions and aversions, singularities and dichotomies that continue to move like a pendulum, now find a central, neutral point of balance.

This neutrality gradually cultivated in the *chitta* finally creates a sense of equanimity that may not yet become manifest at the level of the conscious mind but that nonetheless leaves its power in the unconscious mind, giving a new direction to its hidden tides and undercurrents. A person thus practicing his mantra diligently may, over a long period of time, come in touch with and change the entire pattern of the *samskaras,* and give conscious internal direction to their participation with the practice of meditation and mantra. It is for this reason that the daily practice of meditation as well as special observance of the mantra practice (of which we speak elsewhere) always begin with the recitation of a mental *sankalpa*—declaration of a sacred resolve which goes somewhat as follows:

> On this day, _____ and date, _____, I undertake the resolve to complete _____ recitations, or _____ periods of meditation for the sake of the purification of my being, for the pleasure of my guru, and *nishkama* (seeking no personal benefits for myself). By this observance of mind, may the countless myriad of sentient beings who are in misery and suffering be enlightened and may their suffering be alleviated.

It is only by maintaining this type of attitude that the mantra practice can become an antidote to *karma*. If it is practiced *sakama,* that is with some desire in mind, such as seeking some personal fulfillment, the healing of illness in oneself or in loved ones, the attainment of prosperity, or the overcoming of other impediments in life, then it is simply the addition of a good *karma* to oneself and does not lead to freedom from the bondage of *karma*.

It is for this reason that in many mantras the word *namah* occurs. Although grammarians derive this word from the word *nam,* meaning "to bend" or "to salute," the yoga tradition has its own linguistic memory and says that the word is a shortened form of *na mama,* meaning *"not mine."* In other words, one surrenders one's claims of ego if one wishes to meditate effectively, and that alone constitutes a bowing down in adoration offered to the deity within oneself and to the One within the universe. This same word occurs in the normal greeting between human beings in the Indian civilization when the phrase *namas te* is uttered with the hands clasped before the heart and the head bowed:

> With all the love of my heart, with all the power of action in the hands, with all the thought in the head,

I declare *not mine;* I hereby give up all the claims of
my ego in your honor; I adore and worship the
Deity who is within you.

What a powerful greeting this is when offered in the form of a
mantra within oneself so that all the possessions of the lower
ego are burned in the fire of sacrifice to the divine presence
within.

5

The Meaning of My Mantra

The forceful role that a single word can play in one's psychology and life can be illustrated by paying attention to one's own name. A name is simply a word; one is not born with that name. When you came out of the mother's womb you did not say, "Hi, Mother, I am Sarah!" Someone else decided by what name to address you. You did not know that name, but after a while you realized that every time they said the word "Sarah" they looked at you or they gestured toward you. "That particular sound must have something to do with me," you thought. Gradually you began to associate that sound with yourself, and you realized that that was the name you were supposed to have—for no particular reason at all. In the mind of the others there may be some reason, although it may have absolutely nothing to do with your aspirations. It may be some social customs, family situations, or just a desire to please the great grandfather. Yet this name has made such an impact on you, that you sign it everywhere and you swear by it, saying, ". . . or my name is mud!" You do not want to dishonor your name, and you feel that some act might drag your name down. You are hurt when your name does not appear where it ought to appear.

But remember that that name has absolutely nothing to do with your inner psyche. It was absolutely arbitrarily chosen for you. There was not even a scientific reason for you to have that name, although in the traditions of India even the personal name is given after astrological deliberation. There is a list of sounds with which a child's name should begin according to the planetary position because it is felt that the vibrations of the sounds in a name are attuned to the cosmic vibrations. When the swamis take the vows of swamihood they receive a new name. At marriage, women, and in some cultures men, change their names. The monks and nuns in the Christian tradition are given a sacred name, because it is felt that a new life is beginning, a new attitude must be assimilated into one's thought pattern. So it is obvious that the effect of a word that is often repeated, even in nonspiritual contexts, is recognized in almost all traditions of the world. In certain spiritual traditions, even among the yogis, to give a mantra is termed *naam-dena*, which means "to give a name," and for a disciple to receive a name is called *naam-lena*. This does not mean that the disciple is necessarily given a new name when he or she receives a mantra, but that the mantra has the same or greater force in one's life than even an individual name. When one is deeply asleep, he awakens when his name is called because the name has become deeply ingrained into the subsurface areas of the mind. Likewise, when the mantra begins to take root in those areas, as well as in all the other concealed faculties of the mind, it is then that it becomes most effective.

This brings us to another area of people's inquiry into the mantra. They ask, "What is the meaning of my mantra?" Here let us remember that you love your name and are attached to it, but not because of the way it can be translated, even though the translation may be very meaningful, but because of your association with it, because of a certain impact its very sound carries on your mind. Select, for example, a name arbitrarily; *Theodora* in Greek means "given by God" or "God-given." You may become a complete atheist in life and yet carry the name Theodora, God-given! And you feel no pangs of conscience when signing your name as such. The meaning of the word *Theodora* in the dictionary is "God-given," but in daily life that is not the meaning you associate with it. The meaning of the word *Theodora* is *you*—your whole person is *Theodora*—but that is not what the dictionary says.

The ancient linguists have pointed out that the meaning of a word is not another word in another language, nor is it a series of phrases. The meaning of the word has nothing to do with the way it translates into another language. Take for example the word *water*. If you are a German reading English, what is the meaning of the word *water?* "Wasser." But if you are an English-speaking person reading German, what is the meaning of the word *Wasser?* "Water!" Which then is the word and which is the meaning? And how would one translate either of these words to someone deaf or mute? The Sanskrit word for an object is *padartha*, which means "the meaning of the word." That is to say that words are not the meanings of words; only the objects are the meanings of words. More simply put, the word is the *significator*, and the object denoted is the *significatum*, that which is signified, pointed to. The translation of the words *Theodore* and *Theodora* may be "God-given," but when it is one's own name, oneself alone is its meaning. The word is the *significator*, and oneself is the *significatum*. Without a full understanding of this principle no one is going to be able to understand the meaning of his mantra, and no matter how many translations of the mantra may be attempted they all will be incomplete, unsatisfactory, and misleading.

Words—that is, sounds made by the human larynx—are not entirely different from other sounds made in nature. For example, a song may be sung in a certain tune, and the same song may be reproduced by a musician on a string instrument without any vocal accompaniment. On the other hand a tune thus heard may be given words by a poet, and those words may be sung by a vocalist. What is the relationship between the tune produced by the singer and that by the instrument player? The relationship lies in what is known in Tantra as *nada*, the principle of sound that is not differentiated. Grammarians say that the sound of the words from the human throat or that of notes from a stringed instrument, is *dhvani*, a differentiated sound. Although such sounds are completely different in many ways, yet they have a common denominator, *nada*, the principle of unity in which they both share. This principle of *nada* is expressed by a human *undifferentiated cosmic sound*. It is expressed in Indian music by the presence of a drone instrument such as the *tanpura*, without which not even an expert sitar player can play his music. In the background of his music there must remain the undifferentiated monotone of a drone like that of an ooooommmmm. If one were to take all the sounds of the universe with all their differentiations—from the birds chirping, to the cosmic rays racing through space, from the musicians singing, to supernovae exploding, from ants crawling, to black holes devouring planets with new worlds being created while the old ones are being dissolved, or from fetuses hearing the sounds of the mother's heartbeat and the blood coursing through her veins to the waves breaking on the shores—if all these sounds were simultaneously recorded, there would be only one single sound: ooooommmmm. The drone of that monotonic cosmic sound is the background against which every instrument of the orchestra of the universe plays; it is the Theme on which all the diverse sounds are a variation. It is that line which runs above all the letters of the Sanskrit alphabet, joining them—the line of singularity of the unmanifest, of the oneness of the many in infinity.

It would appear that we have spoken of the objective

sounds of words alone, but what do these external sounds really have in common with the internal meditative principle of *nada?* The *dhvani*, the principle of the external sounds of the objective word, arises as a projection of the *nada*, which is not a sound created through friction, not a fire produced by rubbing two pieces of wood together, but an internal symmetry in consciousness. *Nada* may be called the sound of consciousness from which the consciousness of external sound develops. We repeat: *nada* is the *sound of consciousness* from which the *consciousness of external sound* develops. An ordinary word is simply *dhvani;* it may be arbitrarily replaced by another sound, as is done in translating. But the internal sound called the *nada* cannot be replaced; no substitutes for it can be found.

Let us explain this by the analogy of the sources of knowledge. One source of knowledge is information and the other is intuition. Information is gathered through observation and is fed in through the mind. Through the senses it begins from the many, passes through a variety of channels, and is unified in a singular mental energy, only to the extent that all the various pieces of information have found a single substratum. This requires a logical approach—parts of an equation, members of a syllogism—before drawing a conclusion. The intuitive knowledge, however, is not arrived at through these processes. It is an instant flash coming to the surface of the mind from the hidden resource. It is the unmanifested becoming manifested. It is not perceived part by part, but rather flashes as one entire whole whose parts may be analyzed later.

Nada, the sound of consciousness that the yogis hear, has the same source as that of any other intuitive knowledge. Just as a single *hummm* of the external universal sound is divided into so many pitches, tones and tunes, so the *nada* is divided into inner sonar vibrations called the mantra. And just as intuitive knowledge later finds the words for itself to be conveyed in the form of a logical sequence, so also the *nada* becomes a mantra and may be then produced in the form of *dhvani,* the manifest sound. At this stage it is in the form of syllables and words that appear in no way different from those of the ordinary language. We have seen that even an ordinary word, once becoming associated with consciousness, and once becoming a name, then conveys an experience entirely different from that of the translation. How much more so would the mantra convey a meaning different from a translation since it is not artificially, externally associated with consciousness? It certainly does not develop through the processes applied for conditioning the mind from childhood. Rather, it arises within consciousness itself and is imparted in a way entirely different from that of learning a language or of giving someone a name. Let us elaborate on this a little more.

When an English-speaking person utters the word *water* or a German-speaking one says *Wasser,* they are not using these words as a replacement for each other; they are naming a certain idea, their experience of a given object. When a deaf and mute person wants to express the idea of the same experience he uses sign language. The sign he makes also is not a translation of *water* or *Wasser* or a replacement for these words; it is an independent gesture expressive of the same common experience. A blind person lacks the visual experience of the object but has the experience of its touch, its flow against a finger, its capacity to quench thirst. An articulate blind person may know it as water, but he has less of an experience of the same object. The deaf and mute may not have the articulate word, but he has a greater part of its experience. Thus, the German or the English words as well as the sign all have the same common denominator: the idea of an experience. The *sky* is not *Himmel,* nor is *Himmel* the *sky,* but both words express the idea of the experience one receives when one tilts one's head upwards at a 90° angle. The meaning of both the words *sky* and *Himmel* is the experience of that which stretches from horizon to horizon.

An initiate will not understand the significance of his mantra without abandoning the notion that a translation is the meaning.

Does this mean that the mantras are meaningless sounds? This question can be answered with a cross-question addressed to a music-lover. What is the meaning of Beethoven's Ninth Symphony? Can you possibly translate one of the movements from the symphony into English?! No! Then is the symphony meaningless? No. It is as meaningless—or as meaningful—as one's own name, as we have discussed earlier. Obviously its meaning does not reside in any kind of a translation but simply in a very powerful experience one has upon hearing it. The music is a product of the inner consciousness of an intuitively attuned person who then gave it a sound, *dhvani,* to communicate it to the world. Not all the words in the encyclopedia could express its meaning. At a concert, one can observe a thousand people meditating on the same sound. The process is fourfold: an inner *nada* is heard by the inner ear of a musically trained, intuitive artist. He then transfers it to his musical instrument, producing a *dhvani.* The resonances from the instrument travel and reach the ear of the listener, and as the notes touch the consciousness of the listener they are once again converted into *nada,* into which each listener is absorbed simultaneously along with the thousand others in the chamber. It is thus that a thousand people are listening to an internal *nada,* meditating on the same sound within, and there is a pindrop silence among them.

Here we may digress a moment to answer a question that may naturally arise. Why can we not then meditate on a musical sound? Why a mantra? The answer is, there are indeed ways known to great yogis of meditating with music. In fact all Indian music was an attempt to reproduce the very subtle sounds that were heard inward by the practioners of Nada Yoga, the yoga of sound. It is because these inner sounds are so fine, so subtle, that all Indian music is dominated by quarter tones and microtones. The difference between meditating in a music hall and, on the other hand, with the mantra in a private chamber is simply this: in listening to the music, one is still dependent on *dhvani,* a sound produced externally that causes a remembrance of an internal *nada,* whereas in the practice of mantra one is immediately in tune with the source of music in the inner consciousness. Secondly, in listening to music one hears a series of millions of sounds. While this by itself is a very desirable and enjoyable experience and must be appreciated, it cannot be strictly called a meditation because there is not one single object on which the mind is concentrating, as in the case with mantra. Thus mantra meditation leads to a completely different and higher level of concentration, of awareness.

By now the reader understands why the Sanskrit word for an object is *padartha,* "the meaning of a word." The object, the experience of the object, the idea of the experience, together constitute the true meaning; thus the meaning of one's mantra is that experience to which meditation with the mantra leads. In this way the very meaning of the word *meaning* is altered in the mind of a *sadhaka* and he seeks not the intellectual translation, which in fact will be meaningless, but rather the experience signified by the words of the mantra, the experience to which the practice of the mantra leads.

The universe is a dance and a symphony with many forces, tunes, tones, instruments, playing together in synchronized harmony. The steps are of many dancers, the forces within the universe, all working in unison so that their movement and sound are often indistinguishable from one another. The universe has a multi-level reality—take any object and look at it, and one can find this to be true. Depending on one's place in the audience, the dance is seen from one's own particular angle.

Take any object in the world and try to have the

philosophers and scientists of various persuasions define it. Each one is sure that his definition is the correct one. Take the ordinary table in one's home. What is this object? The simple answer is, "a table," but ask an expert in geometry, and his answer will not be simply a table but he will state and draw the geometric shapes and forms that go into making a table. What is this object? Wood. What is this object? Part of a tree. What is this object? So many living cells that were in this tree. Again, what is this object? Molecules of various organic compounds. Yet again, what is this object? The various atomic and subatomic particles. One more time, what is this object? The whorls and cycles of energy. What is that other object? A saw. And again, through a similar process, the answer is the whorls and cycles of energy. It is a funny kind of energy that takes a saw to cut through! This multi-level reality applies to all objects and all human experience including sound and words.

Levels of Meaning in Mantra

Let us examine here the multi-level nature of the meaning of mantra. We shall explain it by the example of the simple mantra *soham.* This word is used almost universally by the yogis in synchrony with breath awareness. With exhalation, one thinks the sound *ham* (pronounced *hum*). With inhalation, one thinks the word *so.*

Level One-A. The yogis say that this mantra is used in synchrony with the breath because the sound *ham (hum)* is the natural sound of the exhaled breath, as close as the word can get to the sound of the exhaled breath; and the word *so* is the sound one naturally hears during inhalation. Because the sound flows so easily with the breath, it then becomes easier to synchronize the thought to allow a smooth flow of the meditative mind pattern.

Level One-B. However, if you continue to think the

sound *soham, soham, soham,* the first becomes the last and the last becomes the first, as in any universal cycle and all the subcycles. It is an innate principle of nature that the beginnings cannot be discerned from the ends, nor the ends from the beginnings. Where does a circle actually begin or end? So, the sound cycles of *soham* are also experienced as *hamso* or as some schools prefer *hang-so* (pronounced *hung-so.* The explanation regarding the easy flow of the two parts of the mantra with the breath remains the same as in case of *soham.*).

Level Two. For a rationally oriented mind that cannot help but think in the terms of subjects and predicates linked by the verbs of state (e.g., *to be*) or verbs of action (e.g., *to do*), a sentence may be articulated that purports to be the meaning of the mantra. The two parts of the mantra *soham* are (as in One-A above) *so* (by rules of euphony altered from *sah,* pronounced *suh*), simply meaning *he,* or *that;* and *aham* (pronounced *uhum*—both *u*'s as in *u*nder) meaning simply *I,* the first personal pronoun. The verb *to be* is understood. The mantra then means: *I am he* or *I am that.*

Now, you have a translation of the mantra! But did you really get the meaning? Who is that? Who is he? Who is the *I* making the declaration? What is the relationship between the subject and the predicate? In fact, one can ask, which pronoun is the subject and which is the predicate, because it may also be translated as *he is I,* just as well as *I am he.* Philosophers like Shankaracharya, as well as masters in the Tantric tradition, have discussed these questions in many chapters throughout Sanskrit literature, and yet reading all of those philosophical discourses will not impart to the meditator the experience of the true meaning of the mantra.

As we know, the subject of a sentence is that part of speech referring to an object or a person, a qualification of which or a relationship of which is being stated by the predicate. The predicate is that statement. For example, in the sentence,

"John is Sara's husband," "John" is the subject and "Sara's husband" is the predicate. The verb, *to be,* in its indicative present tense third person singular form, *is,* is a verb indicating a state. In "John *loves* Sara," which has a verb of action proceeding from John toward Sara, these three minimum parts—subject, verb and object—constitute a statement or a sentence. Sometimes, however, a predicate may not be articulated. For example we might say, "John is," or, "Cloth is." According to Patanjali in his commentary on Panini's grammar, the definition of a sentence is:

> *Eka-tin vakyam.*
> A sentence is that which contains at least one single verb, whether articulated or understood.

When a verb is not articulated it is sometimes difficult to decide which of the verbs is to be understood. For example, in the mantra *soham,* we are faced with two problems: which is the subject and which is the predicate; and which verb unarticulated here is to be understood. The following interpretations are possible:

> He = I (whatever that means)
> He is I
> I am he

But there is no certainty that the verb forms *is* or *am* are the correct ones. For example, that which is meant might be one of the following:

> He has become I.
> I have become he.

There may be many other similar possibilities, and these alternatives only relate to the *soham* form. But however much one might continue to argue, the problem will not be resolved even after philosophizing and theologizing for one's entire life so that one doesn't have time left to meditate.

It is like the insomniac saying that for all the reading he had to do on the voluminous research on sleep, he simply had no time left for sleep. So, how can one then translate the word *soham?*

This type of discussion is suitable, sometimes, for those on the contemplative path of *viveka* (discrimination) through *vichara,* a well-ordered thought process. It is often used by the adherents of the Vedanta school, not as an indiscriminate pursuit of intellectual curiosity, but rather with the aim of rising to the realization of the transcendental nature of oneself. Then, the intellectual faculty is put to use at the service of the contemplative end.

Yet the Vedantins following the path of meditation itself must use their personal mantras without the intellectual unraveling of these various threads of a single strand. They undertake the observances of well-structured silent contemplation, according to the principles established and well defined in Jnana Yoga, so that in waking hours the intellect is used not in the futile pursuit of intellect for the sake of intellect but for the sake of meditative progress. They finally submerge the intellect into the central core of the mind, and the mind then flows into the transcendental consciousness beyond.

In fact, the best translation, if one simply insists on a translation of the mantra *soham,* would be *He = I* or *I = he.* One is given some help in this by the ancient Vedas, where these shorter mantras occur within the contexts of larger statements. For example, the mantra *soham* occurs in *Yajur Veda XL.17,* which is partly the same as *Isha Upanishad 16.* It states in the Veda:

yo 'sav-aditye purushah so 'sav-aham:

That Person (who shines) in the Sun,
That one I am.

However, the great Shankara, translating the rendering as it
occurs in the *Isha Upanishad,* says:

> *May I be* that Person who permeates the entire
> universe.

Shankara uses *bhavani,* the imperative first person singular
form, to mean, "May I become." Shankara says that the seeker
is certain that one comes to that total realization, and only begs
of the Deity that he may thus become that Person, and, then
finally repeats *asmi,* "I am." In that state of realization the
statement is no longer a prayer nor a wish for any kind of a
change but simply the realization that *I am.*

Level Three. Now we will discuss the next possible level
of the understanding of the *Hamsa* mantra, as the mantra
soham is called. In the circle below it cannot be determined

whether the word written there is *"soham"* or *"hamso."* We have become used to a confined system of language in which, like the Western concept of time, the words are linear; that is, they begin at one point and end at another. But the mantras are a vibration of the infinite consciousness which has no beginning and no end. With *this* in mind, many mantras are practiced— not as though they are merely syllables in which the ordinary rules of language may compel us to look at them.

The simplest example is this one: is the mantra *"soham"* or is it *"hamso"*? The answer is that it is both. In the previous levels of our understanding of the mantra *"soham"* (that is "I am he" or "I am that") the question arises: Who am I? Now, this question, Who am I, is in itself a major contemplation. If one can simply find an answer to this question there is no further need for meditation. In fact, many great yogis, like Swami Rama Tirtha and Raman Maharshi have taught their disciples to contemplate the question *koham,* Who am I? The answer is *soham,* I am that. But *who?* Read the word in reverse and it becomes *"hamso",* which is the answer to the question. The form *"hamso"* is a euphonic alteration, by the rules of Sanskrit grammar, of the word *hamsah.* In other words, the same sound contains the question as well as the answer: I am *hamsah.*

As the realization of one's true nature grows, layer upon layer of one's falsely assumed and externally conditioned indentities begin to drop. At present one says, "I am the body;" later one says, "I am the breath." The first-level meaning of the word *hamsah* is simply the breath: a winged swan of utmost purity. This two-winged swan represents a much purer identity than that of merely a physical body. It is said that in every living being this mantra *soham* or *hamso* continuously throbs unconsciously, and that in each period of twenty-four hours the breath or the heart repeats this mantra 21,600 times.

But the breath is only a vehicle. It is first the vehicle of *prana,* the foremost unit of energy which flows from the sun.

Here we come again to the Vedic affirmation: "The person who shines in the Sun, that one I am."

Only those who have been initiated in the secretmost yoga tradition of solar science fully understand the meaning of the word *hamsah*, for it represents that Sun of life-force with which the yogi finally identifies himself, and the entire *prana* of the universe then comes to be at his disposal. When a yogi reaches this stage he is given the title of *parama-hamsa*—the supreme swan, the supreme Sun, the highest spirit. In the monastic tradition, a swami rises to a point where even the symbols of Swamihood are surrendered into a river and thereafter, no rules of monastic life apply, because, having first renounced all the externals of the world, now he has renounced the renunciation itself. From that moment on he wanders free of the symbols of even his swamihood and is referred to as a *parama-hamsa*. The title is reserved only for those who enter the life of swamihood from celibacy, *brahmacharya*, unbroken through childhood and youth, because they have remained free of the identification with the physical body and the desires of the flesh.

In every Vedantic ashram, a person is awakened with the recitation of *pratah-smarana,* the verses of morning affirmations, the first one of which is as follows:

> At this morning hour I recall
> the essential self flashing in the heart;
> The pure Existence, Consciousness and Bliss,
> the goal and the destiny reached by the *paramahamsas;*
> the fourth, the transcendent state;
> which yet permeates the lower three alterations of
> consciousness, namely,
> the wakefulness, dream and sleep;
> I am that eternal indivisible Brahman;
> I am not this aggregate of elements with which I
> have falsely identified myself.

There are, in the ancient Vedas, another category of mantras whose purport is to explain the short, power-loaded mantras like *hamso.* Here we quote a mantra from the *Yajur Veda:*

> *hamsah shuchi-shad vasur-antariksha-sad,*
> *hota vedi-shad atithir durona-shat;*
> *nr-shad vara-sad rta-sad vyoma-sad*
> *ab-ja go-ja adri-ja rtam brhat.*
>
> *YV.X.24.*

This mantra also occurs in the *Katha Upanishad,* which records the teaching given to young Nachiketas by Yama, the Lord of Death. Here we give a paraphrase of the word-for-word commentary on the mantra by Shankaracharya *(Katha Upanishad, V.2):*

> That *Atman,* the Self, does not pervade only the city of a single body. What then? It permeates the cities of (all the forms of the universe). How so? (Because it is) *Hamsa,* meaning that which reaches, permeates. This *hamsa* is:
>
> *Shuchi-shat*—it dwells in the purest heaven as the Sun-self.
>
> *Vasu*—it is the indweller in all, or, it makes everything to settle.
>
> *Antariksha-sat*—it dwells in the space (of inner vision) as the air-self *(prana).*
>
> It is a priest, the fire,
>
> It dwells in the altar; that is, the earth, for it is said that, "This altar—this point, any given point—is the beginning and the end of the earth."
>
> It is a guest, the *soma,* the spiritual drink that dwells like a guest in its home which is *kalasha,* the chalice (of the body); or it is a wise one staying in the home as a guest.
>
> It dwells within the human beings.

It dwells in the deities.

Rta-sat—it dwells in the eternal law, the universal truth, the universe-sacrifice.

Vyoma-sat—it dwells in the space (of the heart).

It is born in the waters in the forms of all the aquatic beings.

It is born on the earth in the forms of all the edible plants.

It is born (of the universal law) as a part of the sacrifice.

It is born of the mountains as the rivers and the streams, being the self of all or all-self.

Its nature is universal truth.

It is *brhat*—great, because it is the cause of all.

It is the all-pervading one Self of the universe, and there is no differentiation of selves.

If we try to explain the difficult points of the above commentary, that alone will require an entire book, and many lifetimes of contemplation for its assimilation and mental absorption.

Level Four. As one begins to understand that "I am not this body but the eternal spirit," the word *hamsa* then means *sah*—that is *prakrti* or matter, body, flesh—permeated by *ham*—the indwelling spirit. Previously one had identified only with the body, and later with the breath; here now, one sees oneself as a union of the body and soul working together. It is here that one oscillates between the physical being and the spiritual being until the mind begins to settle down yet deeper, and an entry into the *chakras,* the centers of spiritual consciousness, is gained.

Level Five. As explained above, the word *soham* is a euphonic combination of *sah,* or *so,* plus *aham.* The word *aham* in Sanskrit simply means "I." But what does the "I" really include or incorporate? The answer is known to those who are familiar with the system of Kundalini Yoga. The *kundalini,* the divine energy flowing through us, passes through the seven centers of consciousness—this is well known to the students of this spiritual path. The seven centers of consciousness are also the points of the release of the *kundalini* energy into the *prana* and the physical systems, as well as being the inward openings from the psychophysiological personality into the spiritual being. These points of contact between the spiritual energy and the psychophysiological personality are shown in the form of a number of lotus petals in the various *chakras,* the centers of consciousness. To each of these petals is attributed the power of one syllable of the Sanskrit alphabet, fifty letters in all.

As one breathes, in meditative concentration, the *prana* and the mindforce flow along a path of energy which meanders through the various petals of the *chakras.* This is an experiential subject, and those who have not been given the practice will not understand what is being said here. The throat center is the center of sound, containing the syllabic power of all the vowels because the vowels are the support of all the other letters. The first letter of the Sanskrit, Arabic, Hebrew, Greek, Latin or English alphabet is the sound *"a".* In mantra form, it is nasalized to include the *prana* force and is written as *am.* It occurs as the first vowel in the throat center of consciousness. As the mind and *prana* concentration spirals down throughout the various centers to the last letter, it is found that the letter *sa* (written in the *kundalini* system as *sam,* having been nasalized to include the *prana* force) is the last letter in the lowest center of consciousness. This *sah* is the sound that is the farthest from the highest center which is the abode of the Lord, of the spiritual power within us. The word *sah,* therefore, forms, in the spoken language, the pronoun representing "he" or "that", something pointed to as being far away from the abode. But as the *prana* flows upwards again, it is brought to the sixth center, the mind center, where the power of the syllable *ham* is seen.

Thus the *prana* thread goes down through the system and then flows up, forming a rosary-like pattern from *a* downwards and then back to *ham* (see chart on page 117). It forms a loop traveling from the letter *a* in the throat center downwards and back up to *ham* in the eyebrow center, thus forming the word *aham*.

So we see that consciousness moves from the first letter of the Sanskrit alphabet, *a,* to the last letter, *ham,* from alpha to omega, meaning "I". When we say *aham* in Sanskrit we are saying "I", from alpha to omega, from the first sound of the universe to the last, through all the centers of our consciousness, all the aspects of our psychophysiological personality. All this is I, *aham.* And, when we say *soham,* it means that even the most distant of the sounds, those farthest from the highest center of consciousness, even those deep within the loins of the earth, in the lowest centers of consciousness, are permeated by "me;" "I am" even that. And "I am" also that *sah* raising from the lowest center along the paths of the upward-flowing energy through the *prana* in the breath's stream to *ham,* the sixth center of consciousness. Only when all the lower sounds are thus brought to the sixth center and the mind becomes the ruler of the earth, water, fire, air and space, the mastery over which is located in the lower five centers, does the yogi then raise the entire garland of letters, as it has been called, to the seventh center, where all sounds become one.

Here we end our brief discussion of the most common mantra, the word *soham* or *hamso.* Now when a person asks the meaning of his mantra, you can see at what length he would require an explanation, which will certainly not be a simple translation of words. It is only after one has gone through the experience, as described above with reference to the word *soham,* that any explanation itself would become meaningful. The most that can be said to a beginning level initiate is that the mantra (or the syllabic components of the mantra) represents the various rays of infinite consciousness.

6

Revelation
and Inspired Speech

In order for us to apprehend the concept of the rays of consciousness as crystallized in the units of sound, we first need to drink deep of the ancient tradition regarding the meaning and process of revelation. The experience of revelation was held in the highest possible reverence, second only to that of God-realization because it is through the God-realized beings that revelation occurs. In the ancient Vedas, the earliest revealed texts of humankind, and in the subsequent exegetical Vedic literature, the revealed truth is expressed by many different words. First, it exists in the form of *rta*, the universal law as co-existent with divine principle which becomes *satyam*, the truth as known to the human being. The principle of sound expressive of this eternal law is referred to as *vac* or *vak*, the Speech Principle in the universe. When the eternal law is manifest in revelation, the totality of revelation is Brahman, an expansion of consciousness. This Brahman is not to be confused with Brahman as the transcendental God Principle, but rather the revelation of knowledge from this latter. When the Brahman or *vac* is narrowed down and becomes enunciations, these are then known as the mantras and the twenty thousand hymns of the Vedas often extol the mantra. One sage declares:

> We walk and act in accordance with our mantras as
> we have heard them.
>
> *Sama Veda I. 176*

We have read in the *Rig Veda:*

> May mantra be our guru again and again.
>
> *Rig Veda I.147.4*

> This mantra as taught by the wise is true.
>
> *I.152.2*

> An inner fire accepts the mantra lovingly with the
> mind.
>
> *I.31.13*

> The master of revelation (Brahman) recites the
> mantra in which all the deities have made their
> home.
>
> *I.40.5*

> Let us declare this mantra in assemblies as the very
> being of peace.
>
> *I.40.6*

> Let us teach this mantra, beautifully carved from
> our very heart.
>
> *II.35.3*

> Those best of human beings who have carved this
> mantra have overcome the world with their shining
> minds.
>
> *VII.7.6*

> May the mantras taught by the wise protect us.
>
> *VI.50.14*

This fire sitting hidden in the cave supports the shining ones holding in his hand all the minds of human beings. The men bear the wisdom that is found here as they recite the mantras that have been carved from the heart.

I.67.2

Oh Fire, you uphold the earth, you support the heavens with the mantras that are true.

I.67.3

Indra, the bearer of treasures; he, the masterful spirit, again and again becomes the form after form creating *mayas* all around his very self, as he surrounds each moment of heaven thrice with his mantras, drinking without season, the bearer of eternal law *(rta)*.

III.53.8

One bearing three mothers and three fathers yet stays above and no (powers) can pull him down. The wise shining ones on the seat of heaven yonder turn into mantras the speech *(vac)* which knows the universe—yet does not come into the universe.

I.164.10

These are only some of the references from the Vedas extolling the mantras. It will require much contemplation on the part of the reader to match these words with his experience of inner light and personal revelation to understand exactly what is meant in these enigmatic verses. As we translate these words we must bear in mind that we have not indicated the multi-level meaning of each word of these hymns in the same way as the the single word *so-ham* discussed above. It can take a very long time to fully understand and grasp the innermost purport. These words are not spoken by an ordinary mortal.

In eight verses of *Rig Veda X.125*, we are told by *Vac*, the

Principle of universal Inspired Speech, speaking in first person:

> I myself am making this declaration, loved both by
> the shining ones and by the human beings. Whom-
> soever I love, him I make formidable; him I make a
> *Brahma* (Lord of a single universe), a *rishi* (a self-
> realized being through whom revelation may be
> channeled). Him I make a person of beautiful
> intuitive wisdom *(medha)*.
>
>   *X.125.5*

We are told of this revelation in the following words:

> A honeyed wave has swelled up from the
> ocean. It has brought close the enjoyment of the
> ambrosia of immortality with its silent draft hidden
> in secret caves, the name of this burning one, the
> tongue of the shining ones, the navel (the center) of
> the ambrosia of immortality.
>
> These streams flow from the ocean of the
> heart; harmoniously flow the speeches, like rivers,
> being purified with the mind in the interior of the
> heart.
>
> Here come forth the waves of the melting
> one like deer speeding away from the hunter.
>
>   *IV.58.1,5,6*

We are told of this process of inspiration:

> He who has eyes may see; let him who has eyes see.
> The blind will not be aware of it.
> He who may come to know (inspirations)
> will become the father of the father.
>
>   *I.164.16*

In the same hymn the inspired speech is compared in
verse after verse to a cow abundant with milk from whom

I the calf may drink to satiety.

I.164.28

Thereby the immortal may become the twin brother
of the mortal.

Verse 30

I cannot distinguish what it is that I am,
a little infant bound with the mind;
I wonder when the first-born children of truth
will come to me;
Oh, may I enjoy the share of a potion of this
inspired Speech.

Verse 37

That supreme space in the single imperishable
letter (Om) of the inspired Speech,
in which all the gods have settled—
he who does not know that,
what will he do with hymns and verses?
Those, however, who know That One,
they sit here together in harmony.

Verse 39

This fair one measures and carves the waters
(of primordial knowledge), being of a single word,
of two words, of four words, of eight words,
nine words,
desirous of becoming the thousand-syllabled speech
in the supreme space.
    It is from her
that all the oceans wash forth variously,
by which all the four directions come alive.
From that One comes into perishable existence
the Imperishable Letter,
and the whole universe lives by that one word.

Verses 41,42

That breast of yours, so restful and auspicious,
by which you nurture all the beautiful things,

that which holds all the jewels,
that where all the wealth is to be found,
that ever beautifully giving breast,
Oh, flowing One—who will drink of that breast?

Verse 49

It is only those who are well-endowed with the principle of purity who are considered worthy of drinking of this inspiration, of this ever-flowing miracle of divine speech. Elsewhere we are told:

> Someone seeing this speech *(Vac)* does not see her,
> someone hearing her does not hear,
> yet to someone she opens up her body
> as a beautifully adorned loving wife to her husband.
>
> *X.71.4*

And again in the same hymn:

> Equal friends,
> all having the same eyes and ears
> are unequal in the attainments of the mind.
> Some wade up to the ankles, some up to the armpits,
> few are seen coming out
> having taken a full dip in the waters.
>
> *X.71.7*

It is for those who can dive deep that the knowledge concerning the inspired speech is available. The metaphor of waters continues through many centuries. We read in a commentary on grammar:

> Waters are the most purifying of all things on earth,
> yet more purifying than waters are the mantras.
>
> Bhartrhari in commentary on his
> *Vakyapadiya, I.1*

In the Vedic exegesis called the *Brahmanagranthas* we are told at least nine times that

> word is God,
> the speech is God
> whatever is speech is God,
> God is the supreme space of speech,

and so forth.

> *Gopatha I.2.10;*
> *Aitareya II.15; IV.21; VI.3;*
> *Shatapatha II.7.4.10; XIV.4.1.23; XIV.6.10.5;*
> *Jaiminiya Upanishad Br. II.9.6; II.13.2;*
> *Taittiriya III.9.5.5*

There repeatedly occur the metaphors of speech as fire:

> *Taittiriya III.10.8.4;*
> *Jaiminiya I.28.3; II.2.1; III.2.5;*
> *Gopatha IV.11;*
> *Shatapatha I.4.2.17; III.2.2.13; VI.1.2.28*

or, speech as a cow:

> *Gopatha I.2.21;*
> *Tandya XVIII.9.21;XXI.3.1*

or, speech as the ocean, waters, river or flowing stream:

> *Tandya VI.4.7; VII.7.9; XX.14.2;*
> *Aitareya V.16;*
> *Shatapatha VIII.5.2.4*

In this literature, called the *Brahmanagranthas,* alone, there are at least one hundred eighty-four powerful statements about the inspired speech. Perhaps the most succinct one is:

Speech is the feminine principle of the universe.
Jaiminiya IV.22.11;
Shatapatha I.4.4.4; IV.2.1.22

We shall need to refer to this literature again a little later. Some scholars may argue that the references to speech in this literature concern ordinary speech, but we look carefully and find these statements:

The speech verily is the Progenitor's own glory:
Shatapatha II.2.4.4

Prajapati (God as Progenitor) indeed was one
and alone. The speech was his own being.
The speech was the second to him.
He said:
"Let me send forth this speech—
she will go and become all these various things."
So he created, sent forth
the speech to become the various things.
Kathaka-Samhita XII.5.27.1

Prajapati (Lord as Progenitor) was indeed It.
The speech was his Second, the only other.
He had intercourse with Her. She became pregnant.
She went away from him.
She gave birth to all these things.
She returned and again entered the very Progenitor.
Tandya XX.14.2

Elsewhere it is stated:

Speech itself is Lord the Progenitor.
Taittiriya I.3.4.5;
Shatapatha I.6.3.27; III.3.22; V.1.5.6; XII.4.1.15

In other words, the knowledge, the word, is inseparable from God. This idea of the unity of God the Creator and his knowledge as speech becomes clearer when we are told that all the phenomena of the universe are his utterances. He uttered the word *"bhuh"* and created *bhuh,* the earth. As we are also told by the lawgiver Manu (I.21):

> the names of all things—
> he gave from the words of the Veda.

The *Mahabharata (XII.232)* elaborates on Manu's statement, which we present with the commentator Nilakantha's exposition as follows:

> The *rishis* (sages) sought the Vedas through ascetic endeavor day and night.

Nilakantha's exposition:

> They brought to conscious memory, through the power of yoga, the knowledge they already had attained in previous lives (during former cycles of creation).

> The knowledge that is Word (*vac,* speech) without beginning or end, was emitted by the Self-existent Being. The names of the *rishis,* all the creation as (set out) in the Vedas, the multifarious forms of the elements, and initiating of acts, *all these* the Lord creates in the beginning from the words of the Vedas.

Nilakantha's exposition:

> As we read in the texts: "He uttered *Bhuh,* and created the earth"—and so forth . . . . It is to be understood that through the utterance of the relevant word alone the first creation by the divine Being (occurs) and not through the tangibles *(drsh-*

ta) presented *(rupa)* as reminders of a signified meaning *(artha)*.

> There are two aspects of God (Brahman): God the Word *(shabda-Brahman)* and the Transcendental Supreme One.
>
> *Mahabharata XII.232*

About the meaning of the word *mantra* we read in *Mahartha-Manjari (V.48)*, a Tantric text of Kashmir:

> *manana-mani niya-vibhave*
> *niya-sankocha-bhaambhi tranai*
> *kvaliyaa-avisra-viapa*
> *kshana-bhuvi kavi manta-sandatho.*

> Contemplative of Her own expansive glory
> Protective towards (the universe which is), Her own contraction
> Swallowing all polarized mentation (into Her own singularity)
> some such experiential consciousness—
> this is the meaning of the word 'mantra'.

On this a commentator quotes an unknown source:

> A mantra is not composed of letters ... ...
> The heaving of *nada*, the inner subtle sound in a state prior to mentation is called mantra.

The last sentence can also be understood to mean:

> The heaving of *nada*, the primordial sound, in a state just prior to creation of the universe is called the mantra.

Elsewhere we are told:

The mantras that are recited
are no mantras at all.
Without the *immutable potency* that is in the mantras,
as their very life and soul *(jiva),*
they are futile like a cloud that will not rain.

Shiva-sutra-vimarshini

Out of this philosopy developed the fascination of the
ancient teachers with the hidden mysteries of the language and
letters. How old the mantras themselves are cannot be
determined, but the evidence seems to indicate that by the
thirteenth century B.C., the Sanskrit alphabet had already been
scientifically divided, *vyakrta,* into its most modern form. The
fascination with the mystery of language and letters led to later
speculation on phonetics, the earliest seeds of which are found
in very ancient texts. For example, we read:

A (alpha) is the entire speech; diversified in association with the mutes and sibilants (the consonant), it
yet abounds and becomes manifold.

Aitareya Aranyaka II.3.6

In other words, even a single letter of the alphabet such as the
letter *alpha* carries within it the power of the entire manifestation of the universe. Around the eighth century B.C. we read:

These 65 letters (of the Sanskrit alphabet) are the
God-Aggregate, the vocalizations of the very self.

Yajuh-pratishakhya VIII.15

Not merely the unmanifest knowledge hidden in God is
the Word of the Divine Principle, but even the diversified
speech is similarly sacred, inspired as though many sparks of
the fire of God brought together in a single heap creating an
alphabet. Great Patanjali, who is reputed to be not only the
author of the Yoga Sutras but also of the great commentary on

the grammar of Panini (approximately seventh century B.C.), was born somewhere between the fourth century B.C. and first century A.D. We read in his commentary, *Mahabhashya (I.1.2)*, on Panini's grammar:

> This recitation of the letters (of the alphabet) is the very enunciation of speech blossoming and fruitful, adorned beautiful like (the) moon and the stars. This should be known as the very God-aggregate, *Brahman-rashi.*

On this, a later commentator, Kaiyata, says:

> the very essence that is Brahman (God) shines forth in the form of words.

The greatest epic of the world, the *Mahabharata,* states that:

> He who is immersed in the Word that is God *(Shabda-brahman)* attains the Supreme Brahman.
> *Critical edition, Poona,*
> *XII.224.10; XII.262.1*

All the various forms of speech are thus regarded, as we saw in the hymns of the Vedas, as waves arising from a single ocean, appearing manifold and yet maintaining one reality. Thus, all the letters and words are united in the single Speech Principle, the Word that is God, the knowledge of the divine being in the manifest universe and in the transcendental supreme reality. We read:

> As the crystal is a pure substance, yet in association with various colors may appear separately blue, red, yellow and so forth (so in single Speech Principle various letters and words make their appearance).

Unknown ancient text quoted by Madhava in his
Sarva-darshana-sangraha in the chapter on the
philosophy of grammar.

Just as the various letters and words are manifestations
of the single divine Speech Principle, so a single word may
contain within itself the power of the entire Principle. Thus we
read again from Patanjali, in his work on grammar:

> One single word fully known with the authority of
> the texts and scriptures, properly applied, fulfills all
> one's desires.
>
> *Mahabhashya VI.1.84*

That single word could be a single letter; for example, the letter
A (alpha) as stated above, or the most powerful of the mantras,
the word *Om*, about which another grammarian, Bhartrhari,
says:

> This word is the root nature of all words and their
> meanings.
>
> *Vakyapadiya I.10*

7

Subtle Origins of Sounds

The vast number of schools of the study of phonetics, linguistics, grammar, etymology and the related sciences which were developed in ancient India and whose methods, findings and scientific enunciations have not yet been excelled even in modern times, all developed from the fascination of the ancient sages with the power of the word. They knew that *Shakti,* the feminine energy of the universe, was the divine power inherent in the word. The teachers of Tantra expounded in great detail a complex theoretical framework in which a person may undertake a journey of consciousness to trace his steps from the ordinary spoken word, upwards and inwards to the subtlety of the source of all speech, the universal energy.

The philosophers of the Mimamsa school altogether ignored the questions such as the existence of God, and occupied themselves with proving the eternity of the Word itself. The yoga system itself is concerned with the practical ways of enhancing the consciousness. The Vedanta school explained how the one infinite Brahman creates from within Itself many words that become the phenomena of the universe, one phenomenon being speech itself. The philosophers of grammar took up this very theme and, throughout the history of Indian philosophy, aligned themselves with the Vedanta system. That is why we find that even the earliest grammarians echo the word of the *Upanishads* and the later grammarians use words such as *vivarta,* the "whirl," to explain the phenomenalization of the single universal Speech Principle.

The greatest grammarian of any language ever born was Panini. Although the exact dates of his life are unknown, he definitely lived before the seventh century B.C. He systematized and codified the entire Sanskrit language in four thousand aphoriams *(sutras).* His commentator, Patanjali, implies that Panini sat in meditation when composing the *sutras,* thus receiving them while in a superconscious state.

The first fourteen *sutras* simply enunciate the letters of the alphabet. It is to be remembered that the Tantra writers speak of the letters of the alphabet as *matrkas,* little mothers of the Universe, because of their vibration. The tradition has it that Panini's consciousness picked up these first fourteen aphorisms *(sutras).* His commentator, Patanjali, implies that Lord Shiva himself at the end of his dance of creation. More simply put, the very origin of the human alphabet, when it is received as a revelation in a higher state of consciousness, is nothing but the diversification of the very first sound waves that are sent forth into the universe at the time of creation.

There had already been at least a dozen grammarians and etymologists before Panini's time whose systems were modified and incorporated in his own codification. Although Panini himself did not go into philosopical statements concerning the origin and the beauty of revealed word, his entire life points to the fact that the language itself was regarded by him as a revelation.

Patanjali, in order to state the purpose of the study of grammar, quotes the Vedic hymn (171.4), referred to above:

We study grammar so that this speech may open herself up like a loving wife to her husband.

Patanjali says that

this great celestial principle, *mahan devah,* the Word, *shabda,* though immortal, has entered us mortal beings.

From the time of Patanjali, approximately the fourth century B.C., the philosophers of grammar became more and more concerned with the questions elucidating the relationships of the human mind with the divine, eternal Speech Principle.

Here we quote from Bhartrhari, a philosopher of language who was born sometime before 450 A.D. He divided his text into three cantos: the first canto is on Brahman *(Brahma-kanda),* the second on words, the third on sentences. But it is the first that is of greatest interest to us here. Some verses from this are paraphrased below, explaining the philosophy of the *Shabda-Brahman,* the word that is God, coming into ordinary speech.

1.   The beginningless and endless God *(Brahman),* the
        Word-Principle, imperishable,
      which becomes that manifold whirl *(vivarta)*
        from which the process of the universe commences;

2.   Which is stated (in the text and tradition) as One,
        (yet) divided in association with (many) powers *(shaktis);*
      which, though inseparable, also operates in separate (forms and manners)
        because of the many powers *(shaktis);*

3.   Resorting to whose power of time *(kala-shakti),* with aspects *(kalas)*
        unimpeded,
      the six modifications, the birth, etc., are the origins

of the divisions (that occur in the principle of) Being;

4.   Which is that One seed of all, whose (three fold) mode as this
       (universal phenomenalization),
       is a state (as it takes the) forms of enjoyer, object of
       enjoyment, and (the experience of) enjoyment itself;

5.   That revealed Word (Veda) is well stated (in the tradition)
       by the great sages *(rishis)* as both
       the way to attain Him, as well as His (very) image;
       Though One, it is taught severally
       as though (divided into) many paths.

9.   Its true purity is said there (in the traditions) to be the
       entire knowledge
       whose text is a single word,
       apt, as *Om,* not controverted
       by any doctrine.

We paraphrase the above verses for the sake of clarity.

1.   The Word-Principle is Brahman, God Itself,
       imperishable, beginningless, endless;
     It makes the manifold appearances,
       like water becoming many whirlpools,
       and from It alone the process of the Universe
       commences.

2.   According to the texts and the traditions It is
       One, Indivisible,
     yet, becoming divided in association
       with Its own many powers
       and then operating in many forms and
       manners.

3.   One of its unassailable aspects is the
       power called Time *(kala-shakti)*
     When the single *being* becomes associated with this
       power of time, there originate six divisions of being.

This was explained by sage Yaska, the etymologist, a thousand years before Bhartrhari, as follows:

The single being, *bhava,* is then divided into six modifications through the cycles of time. An object

is born; then it
is; from this moment it
changes; in the ascending cycle of its being it
grows; in the descending cycle it
diminishes, and finally in the sixth state
vanishes.

All phenomena go through these six states, all other states being the modification of these which are alterations in the single state of *being.*

The language also follows the same principle. According to the Vedantins, Brahman produces the manifold phenomena, the objects, as *vivartas,* whirlpools in the waters of Consciousness. According to the philosophers of etymology and grammar, the science of Word *(shabda-shastra),* Word that is God, has one *bhava* or single being which goes through the *vivarta* (whirlpooling) of a variety of verbs expressive of the states of being. Language is divided into two sections:

Names: which are the names of all the objects, phenomena, of Brahman's dividing Itself into many, and

Verbs: expressive of the above six states of being through which the objects pass.

Like One Brahman, and One Word-Principle identical with It, there is only one verb: *to be.* When God touches it to Its power of time, it *becomes,* dividing sixfold as enumerated above. All the other verbs, about two thousand basic ones in Sanskrit language, are expressive of further subdivisions of these six processes.

4. *Shabda*-Brahman, God the Word-Principle, is that
    One seed of all whose three fold modification
    produces the phenomenalization in the Universe.
    This phenomenalization is a state in which the One
    takes the three forms as the
        experiencer,
        object of experience, and the
        experience itself.

5. The great sages state repeatedly in the traditions
    that the revealed Word (Veda) is both the
    way to attain Him as well as His very image.
    Though this revealed word is One, it is taught
    as divided into several sections, many paths.

9. The true purity of the revealed Word is
    emphasized in the tradition quite aptly
    to be manifest in one single word,
    Om, which cannot be controverted by any doctrine.

We continue with Bhartrhari's text.

12. The supreme flavor and essence of speech,
        when it has been divided into forms (and paradigms),
    is this (science of words), the straight path
        (leading) to That which is the sacredmost
        light (of God).

16. This is the first rung among
        steps on the ladder to attainment *(siddhis)*;
    this is the straight royal course for those
        who are about to be liberated *(mokshamana).*

18. This is the best aspect of speech
        when its divisions have been dissolved—
    (so) that in this very darkness (of phenomenalization)

the pure light makes its (manifold)
appearances.

(One does not need the proof of sense-perception or logical
processes of inference to support these statements:)

37. The knowledge of past and future occurs to
     Those (masters) to whom illumination has appeared
     and whose minds are unperturbed—
     their knowledge of past and present
     is no different from the (ordinary people's)
     sense-perception (of present objects).

38. They who see with a seer's eye
     all states that are beyond the senses and
     not (ordinarily) apprehended—
     their word cannot be challenged (on the grounds of)
     any inference.

42. It is easy to be fallible when one's (main) dependence
     is on inference,
     (for he is) like a blind person running on an
     uneven path (and) feeling his way by hand.

46. As the light hidden in a piece of kindling
     (serves as the) cause of a
       different illumination (that of fire),
     similarly, the word hidden in intelligence
     (serves as the) cause of separate sounds.

47. First contemplated through intelligence, and
     then applied to some signification
     It is then grasped *(anu-grh)* as a sound
     produced by the senses of articulation.

131. The Word hidden within is the speaker's
      very *atman*, the spiritual self
      the great excellent one with which
      union is enjoyed.

132. The purification of the word is the very
     siddhi, attainment of God, the Supreme Self.
     He who knows the secret of this process,
     attains the immortal *(amrita)* Brahman.

These statements of Bhartrhari can be understood only when the doctrine of *sphota* is understood. What Bhartrhari means to say is that the variety of words and sounds as experienced in the phenomenal world actually remain one in their essence in the field of consciousness. The process by which the universal consciousness emits the sounds and the words is called *sphota.* This word has been variously translated as sound-essence or sound explosion, depending on the way you look at this principle.

The doctrine of *sphota* is an ancient one, the name of whose founder has been lost in antiquity, although his opinion was quoted by Panini *(VI.1.123)* in the seventh century B.C. where he is simply named Sphotayana, meaning the one who took to *sphota!* Another sage philosopher named Vyadi following Panini but before Patanjali wrote a text dealing with *sphota.* The text was in 100,000 verses (see Patanjali's *Mahabhashya I.1.1* and *II.3.66* commentaries). In it, Vyadi examined fourteen thousand different topics, but the work vanished, perhaps before the fifth century A.D.

However, the doctrine of *sphota* was so powerful that almost every school of philosophy discussed its *pros* and *cons* and many philosophers such as Bhartrhari (before 450 A.D.), Mandana Mishra (eighth century A.D.) and Nagesha (eighteenth century A.D.) composed treatises on it or discussed the subject in great detail. The principle of *sphota* is summarized by Professor S. Radhakrishnan as follows:

> According to it any single letter, *c, o, w,* or all the letters, *"cow,"* can not produce the knowledge of the thing corresponding to the word, since each

letter perishes as soon as it is produced . . . There must be something over and above the letters by which the knowledge is produced, and that is the *sphota,* or the essence of sound revealed by letter, word or sentence. This sound-essence produces the cognition of the thing . . . . (A) sentence is the beginning of speech, while words are part of the sentences, and letters are parts of words. *Sphota,* or sound-essence, is said to be eternal and self-existent, bearing a permanent relation to things signified by it.

> *Indian Philosophy Volume II*
> (Allen & Unwin Pub.) 1962 edition, p. 106.

Patanjali says:

The words have sound *(dhvani)* and *sphota* but sound alone is noticed ... ... As the (sound of the) beat of a drum, after it has occurred, reaches sometimes twenty steps, sometimes thirty and sometimes forty; the *sphota* (of it) is the same but the extension is caused by the sound.

> *Mahabhashya I.1.70*

Sphota is of two kinds—internal and external. The internal *sphota* is that explosion of sound-essence that occurs in *samadhi,* the highest state of consciousness, by which the knowledge of Brahman the Supreme Spirit is transferred into *atman* the individual spirit, and is further passed on to the individual intelligence, *buddhi.* By the same process, knowledge is also transferred from the guru's consciousness into that of a disciple. This first transference produces a silent *matra,* an inaudible presence which then manifests itself as *Om.* On this *sound-seed* we can write another detailed book, but suffice it to quote here:

Om: this is the entire speech. Diversified in

association with mutes and sibilants—the consonants—it becomes manifold and of multifarious
forms.

Aitareya Brahmana III.6.7

The experience of this sound passes from the will of pure
intelligence into the subtlest aspect of mind where it then
subdivides itself into *A, U, M*. It is thus that so many unrelated
alphabets begin with the vowel *A (alpha, alef)*. This vowel is the
mother of all articulated sound, as was stated in *Aitareya
Aranyaka II.3.6*. Some philosophers of the mantra science,
especially those of the Tantra tradition, believe that *M* uttered
with closed lips is the first sound manifested from the
unmanifest *Om,* because it is closest to silence, but we need not
go into these controversies here.

The principle of the rudimentary *sphota* is manifest in
the way in which the children learn their first language. In a
spoken sentence the words are not seen apart from the complete
sentence. A sentence like "Give me the toy" is heard as a single
unit of thought. Only because the units such as "give", "me" and
"toy" recur separately again and again elsewhere, does the
child's mind begin to acknowledge these as separate words. The
child's consciousness demonstrates its closeness to the unmanifest, the unitary seed of consciousness, until it becomes
entangled with the plurality of the manifest, objective world.

The same principle is stated more formally in the theory
of knowledge according to Vedanta. This theory states that
human perception passes gradually from the unitary experience
to a plurality; from *nirvikalpa,* the unspecific, to *savikalpa,* the
specific; from indeterminate to determinate. For example, in
the mind of someone looking for his brown horse, these
pictures flash successively:

something
something moving

something moving on four legs, an animal
a horse,
a brown horse,
my brown horse.

Or, someone waiting for the Number Six city transport bus
thinks of:

a vehicle,
a truck—not of my interest,
a car—not what I am waiting for.
a bus—but Greyhound instead of a city bus
a city bus—but not for my route
My bus!

Thus from the general, unitary, all-inclusive perception of *a vehicle,* the awareness then slowly narrows down to a specific part, *one* of many aspects that were hidden, unmanifest in the singularity of the first flash. The mind moves from the non-qualitative universal *(nirguna)* to qualitative particular *(saguna).*

The meditative process reverses this succession, from the plurality of particulars to the singularity of a *bindu,* that one point of consciousness in which *all* the various aspects of the objective world merge, just as they first arose from that very source.

The mantra serves as the way of entering the *sphota* from plurality to singularity, from the multiplicity of thoughts in the mind to a single center.

For those whose minds are pure, *antar-vrtti,* spiritually developed, the *sphota* of *Om* in the consciousness continues on in the process of further revelations. All the energies, powers, and rays of consciousness within it show themselves to the yogi's interior mind in the form of vibrations which, when

brought to the conscious mind, are articulated as mantras.
For the minds that are worldly-bound, the revelations
simply become speech patterns. However, the underlying unity
of consciousness is never really lost. Again, we paraphrase from
the *Brahman-canto* of Bhartrhari's *Vakyapadiya,* a text often
quoted as authoritative by many subsequent philosophers:

71. Even though there be division into words, the oneness
     of all letters is not lost;
     In the different sentences, yet a singularity of words
     is apprehended.

72. There is no word that exists differentiated in
     separate letters;

73. There are no letters in a word, no constituent
     parts in a letter;
     There is no discrimination of words out of a sentence.

The philosophers of the Sanskrit language explain this principle called *sphota* as one by which the process of articulation
occurs through the inner consciousness releasing bursts *(spho-
tas),* of energy in which the unity pervades. Even in the case of
an articulated sound, the *sphota* itself is not subject to time
divisions. Only the lower mind, the senses and the mechanical
sources of sound are subject to time division. Says Bhartrhari,

103. In a minute or a big sound, the time of *sphota* is
      not differentiated. It is the chain of sounds,
      later, that increases or decreases.

Those who have learned to observe the arising of speech from
the will of the spiritual self will comprehend what is being said
here. Even closer to the truth are those who have experienced
the mantra arising as a vibration in various centers of

consciousness. Bhartrhari writes the following concerning *sphota:*

112. This principle internally born subtle, remaining within the word-self *(vac-atman)* manifests itself out in manifold whirls in the form of words, in order to reveal its individuations.

113. It then comes to the state of mentation, thereafter it comes to maturity through *tejas,* the illumination; then it enters *prana* (and) the air, and is then articulated.

114. The air (or *prana*), depending on the element of the internal organ (the mind), possessed by its attributes (of mentation), becomes manifold through the illumination.

115. The *prana* breaking up its knots through the various types of the divisions of sound, expresses the letters, and then dissolves into the very letters.

To simplify:

• The seed of knowledge bursts into the *atman,* the spiritual self,

• *Atman,* through its will, infuses it into *buddhi,* the faculty of intelligence.

• The process of mentation is begun; the *buddhi* is agitated, vibrant.

• The syllables are thought, becoming mantra or secular words.

• The mind awakens *tejas,* the illuminatory power that runs the entire personality systems.

• This *tejas* impells the *prana* which moves the air.

• The air pressed through the organs of articulation becomes the spoken word.

• The volume or the force of the spoken word may vary but

sphota, the process of consciousness, is an invariable constant.

It is the union of the Word-Principle and *prana* that produces speech. Explaining this revelation of mantras, the ancient sages have said:

> Homage to speech, the wife of *prana.*
> *Shadvimsha-brahmana II.9*

> Speech and *prana* are the couple.
> *Shatapatha I.4.1.2*

> Speech is the wife of air *(prana).*
> *Gopatha II.2.9*

> The speech is air.
> *Taittiriya I.8.8.1;*
> *Tandya XVIII.8.7*

> All the *pranas* are established in speech.
> *Shatapatha VII.8.2.25*

> *Prana* is the flavourful essence of speech.
> *Jaiminiya I.1.7*

> So long as there are waters (streams of energy) in
> the *prana* one is able to speak.
> *Shatapatha V.3.5.16*

In the above passages, is speech the function of *prana* or is *prana* the essence of speech? When one is in the process of articulating, moving from within outward, the speech is a function of *prana,* but when one is using the mantra to take speech to its origin, one is moving from coarser to finer, from body to essence. Then *prana* may very well be called the flavourful essence of speech, which is the "husk." The same applies to the relationship between mind and speech:

Mind and speech, among the deities (senses)
are the couple.

Aitareya V.23

For the outwardly conscious,
Speech is the mind's aqueduct.

Jaiminiya I.58.3

But truly
Speech is inferior to mind.
Mind is, as it were, unlimited;
Speech is, as it were, limited.

Shatapatha

Thus, for the inwardly conscious:

Mind is the (ruling) deity of speech.

Jaiminiya I.59.14

Speech is supported by mind.

Shatapatha III.2.4.11

Speech is but mind.

Jaiminiya IV.22.11

So a meditator observes the relationship of the articulated word with *prana,* and even subtler, with the mind. As he goes even deeper, he declares to himself:

yunajmi vacham saha suryena
I yoke the speech to the Sun.

Tandya I.2.1

As he returns the articulated mantra, through silence, to its spiritual origin, he finds,

This speech is the sun itself.

Shatapatha X.5.1.4

The Sun of pure Consciousness will dawn on whomsoever has mastered the pathways for returning articulate diversified speech to its deeper origins in the Word-Principle. This is the purpose of the practice of *japa*, mental recitation of mantra, which we shall discuss later. The same principle is much more elaborately explained by the philosophers postulating the fourfold unfoldment of speech. The four states of the progression from the Word-Principle to articulate speech are called:

> *para:* the supreme one
> *pashyanti:* the seeing one
> *madhyama:* the middle one
> *vaikhari:* the articulated utterance

To define the above, we paraphrase the statements of some of the Tantra texts of the Kashmir tradition; namely,

> *Spanda karikas* of Kallata
> with Ramakantha's commentary IV.18
>
> > SKR
>
> *Shiva-drshti* of Somananda
> with Utpaladeva's commentary II.1-11
>
> > SDU
>
> *Vatulanatha-sutras*
> with Ananta-shakti-pada's commentary VII.
>
> > VSA

It is noteworthy that almost all major authors on the subject quote from Bhartrhari's *Vakyapadiya* and from his own commentary *Svopajna* on the *Brahman-canto* (BVPS). Now we summarize this philosophy:

Para: The Transcendental-Word-Principle in God

(*Brahman, parameshvara, parama-Shiva* etc.).

It is through God's awareness of the illumination of
his own being and the transcendental power *(shakti)* that the Word-Principle is extended. As is said:

If the knowledge were to abandon its eternal form
as the Word-Principle, no (divine) illumination
would illuminate, for she (the Word-Principle, speech)
is the one who cognizes, knows.

Bhartrhari I.124

This is the state of total non-division *(atyanta-
abheda)*

SKR

Those who uphold the non-duality of the Word-
Principle tell us that the Supreme Brahman is
beginningless and never diminishes. That is the
indestructible one (*akshara,* a syllable) in its word-
aspect. That very one is she, the all-seeing Transcendental Speech.

SDU

She is by nature the expansion of the first vibration,
just barely mobile, (i.e., like an almost still ripple) in
the transcendental space which is without waves,
without a veil, without anything intermediate, with
nothing beyond. She holds within herself the
system of the (consciousness of) syllables as non-
dual in a great coalescence, like the undifferentiated
colors of a peacock in a peacock's egg:

VSA

Briefly, *para* is the knowledge as it exists within the ultimate
consciousness of God. It represents the unity of all powers of
will, knowledge and action. The phenomena, the objects, the
names and the sounds of those names have not yet appeared in

any diffusion of multiplicity, but dwell in the singularity of a great coalescence. In a yogi *para* dwells in the thousand-petal lotus.

Pashyanti: this power becomes the *kundalini* in individuated beings. She descends to the *muladhara* and the *svadhisthana chakras.* The individual being experiences a presence of energy which vibrates between the lowest and the highest centers. The divine consciousness has become individuated. In other words, the divine knowledge is being infused into the *jiva,* the spirit of individual life and consciousness. At this stage the mantras are a pure vibration without yet a distinction into syllables.

> This entire multi-phenomenal universe with its divisions and sequences has flashed within (the consciousness). It is yet gathered together, from a state of non-cognition into the space of the nature of consciousness. Her own glory is devoid of divisions and sequences. Here she encloses (the diverse phenomena), enfolds them and maintains nothing but the illumination of her own nature.
>
> SKR

In other words the seed of the phenomenal universe has been planted into her womb but the branches and twigs and fruits have not yet come into being.

> She still sees the inner Supreme Knower
>
> SKR

and is therefore called *pashyanti,* the seeing one. The seeds of the phenomenal consciousness are there, but the true awareness is inward. The world and the physical body have not yet *un*folded. They lie *en*folded in consciousness.

> Without division is *pashyanti,* the seeing one,

> having all the sequences (withdrawn into herself)
> from all directions;
> Her light only on her own nature, inwards,
> she is the subtle speech, that does not diminish
> —is never lost
>
> SKR from BVPS

Of the three powers of God, *viz,* will, knowledge and action which dwell undifferentiated in *para, pashyanti* is called a seer, as God sees all knowledge inward. Without reaching here an ordinary mortal does *not* become a seer.

> When *(para)* takes the form of the unstruck sound *(anahata-nada),* her nature is yet undivided. She holds within herself the (power of the) appearance of all syllables (of mantras), like an entire banyan tree in the banyan seed.
>
> VSA

Jnana-Shakti, the power of knowledge, crystallized in this seeing state, then brings into focus the will, *iccha-shakti,* to distinguish the phenomena that are lying within itself. *Nada,* the universal sound, is then heard in the heart center. It becomes, first, the sound of *Om.* As the diffusion of transcendental light and sound continues to occur the strings of *kundalini* produce an inner music. What a "light and sound show" that is! It is thus that all music began. The music diversifies and the nine inner sounds (or, some texts say, seven: or 9 x 7 = sixty-three) appear. All great traditions of the yoga philosophy of language have given the order in which the sixty-three letters begin to appear one by one. This brings us to the next stage.

Madhyama: At this stage the Word-Principle becomes a state of intellect and mentation. The *kundalini* awakens the mind, and sends into it the vibrations from the various centers of consciousness. The differentiated syllables become the units of thought. Each syllable of the mantra bears within it a ray of consciousness, a certain power, which becomes a particular psychic aspect. The knowledge revealed to the soul has been infused into the mind.

> As the activity of (the universal) *prana* becomes distinct with regard to each individual *prana*-endowed living being, in his body she appears as a sound that is beginningless, eternal, self-risen. She follows on, extends herself, as the sequences of time and divisions of syllables are about to arise . . .

> > Only drawn into intellect *(buddhi),*
> > pursuing the sequential form,
> > passing through the operations of *prana*-
> > the *madhyama* speech functions. (BVPS)
> >   SKR

> She has now arrived at and accepted the ground of determinative intellect which bears resolves and doubts, decisions and indecisions. Here she holds the mass of syllables within herself like nuts in a pod.
>   VSA

At this point the yogi experiences a stirring within himself. The *sphota,* the explosion, the bursting forth of the Word-Principle, from divine to spiritual and from spiritual to mental plane, awakens the *prana.* The mantras at this stage of experience cause a surge of the *prana*-wave which must then impel the airs of breath within the body to serve as vehicles between mind and *prana* on one hand and the sense of articulation on the other.

Vaikhari: Impelled by mind and *prana* the airs, divided into the areas of heart, throat, palate, etc., become the spoken word. Silence is now broken.

To summarize:

God the Word: *para*
Knowledge into soul and *kundalini:*   *pashyanti*
Speech as inspired mentation through
  mind and prana: *madhyama*
Articulated mantra: *vaikhari*

Some yogis have explained it thus:

para:	in *asamprajnata samadhi*
pashyanti:	in *samprajnata samadhi*
madhyama:	in a mental concentration
vaikhari:	in communication.

To recapture Vatulanatha's similes: in *para* the diversity is as unmanifest as colors of a peacock's plumage in a peacock's egg, yet they are all potentially there. In Word that is God, the world, its phenomena and their names are all concealed in that manner.

In *pashyanti,* as divine knowledge is being transfused into the individual spirit, the knowledge of the phenomena and the distinctive syllabic sounds exist like fruits in a seed.

In *madhyama,* the manifestation is diversified like many nuts in a single pod, the syllabic knowledge now remains in the mind and has become sequential. Intuitive wisdom now gives way to rationality. The mantras are mental vibrations, and gradually become thoughts, affecting *prana.*

In *vaikhari,* the fruits, branches and twigs of language and words are all seen separately and one has to search for some semblance of unity behind them.

The Tantric texts insist, however, that the appearance of sequence in the above scheme must be overcome. A true seeker sees the revelation as a spontaneous and instantaneous process. As a piece of iron serving as an iron chest remains molecules of iron which maintain their atomic structure, which in turn remain whirls of pure energy, so *para,* the transcendent, remains ever the same. For those living in a world of time and space, a sequential process seems unavoidable but in the eyes of the seer, *sphota* remains the indivisible constant, ever-present, for

> it is the marvelous supreme pedestal
> of the triple speech,
> divided into many channels
> as *para, pashyanti* and *madhyama.*
> > *Vakyapadiya I.143*

Patanjali says

> *Jyotirvaj jnanani bhavanti*
> The (communications of) knowledge are like a
> flame of fire.
> > *Mahabhashya I.4.29*

This sentence is explained further by commentators Kaiyata and Nagesha to mean that, even though a flame of fire produces light in minute sequential bursts there remains a continuity of light. The knowledge being conveyed appears to be coming in the form of sequential bursts of words and syllables, like so many atoms, yet an inner principle of their eternal unity remains operative. Because, quotes Nagesha,

> Now, this internal knower,
> Subtle, remaining as Word the Self,
> In order to express his own Nature
> Manifests as the whirls of so many words.
> > *Vakyapadiya I.112*

A seeker does not easily become a seer. He must traverse the path that the Word-Principle has taken to become an oral utterance. He must take the uttered mantra and go upstream along the river Sarasvati, the river of speech, the goddess of wisdom.

As the mantra is refined the seeker goes from *vaikhari* to *madhyama,* then to *pashyanti,* where silence is indivisible. On this journey of inward exploration to the origins of his being he discovers that

> Sequence is born from *nada* (the unstruck sound of
> the heart center)
> but *nada* itself is neither an anterior nor a posterior;
> Insequential, it makes an appearance of sequence
> as though it has become divided.
>
> *Ibid. I.48*

At this point the mantra ceases to be a composition of words and syllables. *Madhyama* begins to merge into *pashyanti:*

> There are no syllables in a word,
> nor any parts in a letter;
> Nor can any words be distinguished
> at all in the sentences.
>
> *Ibid. I.73*

When sequences merge into an eternal instant

> She, the Supreme Transcendental Word,
>   that never diminishes,
>   is the light to Her own Nature.
> When Her true aspect is seen
>   all (other) authority retreats.
>
> *BVPS I.143*

In other words, the highest mantra *Om* comes as close as possible to the Word-Principle in God's Consciousness, representing all His powers, all the rays of consciousness. It is in this form that the seed of all sounds exists in the depth of human intelligence. It is only when the intelligence is pulled outwards, downwards, and into the realm of the senses of articulation that it emits nouns and verbs and, as the philosophers of Tantra claim, the mantras specific to the rays of consciousness.

Both the sound *(nada)* and the Word-Principle *(Shabda-Brahman)* exist originally in consciousness as one universal undivided point. Only in association with the realm of phenomena does it become "many," and divide into numerous sounds and words. We are told by the philosophers of language allied with the Vedanta philosophy, that the Word-Principle is *nitya,* eternal. The very first sentence, *varttika,* of Vararuchi, who was the first commentator on Panini's grammar says:

> *siddhe shabdartha-sambandhe*
> The words, their significations and the relationship
> between the two are eternal.

8

Finite and Infinite

Many questions arose and were discussed in three
thousand years of the philosopy of language. One of the
questions was: if the sound is eternal, why does it arise and
vanish? The earliest scientists regarded space to be the *locus* of
sound:

> *akasha-deshah shabdah*
> Patanjali's *Mahabhashya I.1.2*

The sound that dwells in and arises from the space of
consciousness, *chid-akasha,* is eternal. The sound that is
produced through the air-waves impelled from the body into
the material space, *bhutakasha,*

> *akasha-vayu-prabhavah sharirat*

may be considered transient. But even this compromise which
suggested the transience of the Word-Principle was not accept-
able to Patanjali, who was first a yogi and then a master of the
philosophy of sound, word and language. He said:

This alone is not the definition of *eternal:*
"constant, absolute, unmoving; without loss, addition or alteration; unborn, never increasing, of
imperishable association."

Even that is eternal in whom the essence *(tattva)* is
never lost.

What do you mean by essence?

Simply, *being that* (being itself).

Even though the individual (word and sound may
appear to be transient) the (eternal) essence, being
itself, is never lost.

Mahabhashya I.1.1

The commentator Kaiyata said on this as follows:

"There are three types of non-eternity or transience.
One, transience by association, for example reflection of a color into pure crystal. Two, transience in
alteration or modification, for example, a jujube
berry ripening from green into red. Three, transience seen as annihilation."

The first chain of definitions elaborated by Patanjali
precludes the possibility of these three types of transience in the
Word-Principle. "Even that is eternal in whom the essence is
never lost," stated Nagesha. This applies to Brahman in whom
the six modes of becoming *(bhava-vikaras)* enumerated below,
i.e.,

is
is born
modifies
grows
diminishes
vanishes,

do not apply. Each of the attributes of eternity in that definition, one by one, precludes these six modes of becoming. However, there remains the question regarding the appearance of these six modes of transience in the spoken word as it is produced, is heard, and vanishes. Patanjali says that in spite of such an external appearance the essence, the Word-Principle, remains unchanged. The Sankhya philosophers will concur, saying that nothing ever perishes, merely changes its form and is therefore eternal in essence.

Sat, the Principle of Eternal Existence in Brahman, God, carries within it

> *iccha,* will
> *jnana,* knowledge
> *kriya,* action.

When Brahman's *will* initiates *vivarta,* projecting the whirls and whorls of universe and phenomena in their unities or in their diversities, naturally the six fold *action,* or modifications of being with innumerable subdivisions, are given names and verbs to signify them from the *knowledge* of Brahman.

> *jyotirvaj jnanani bhavanti*
> (These) knowledges are like light.*
> Patanjali's *Mahabhashya I.4.29*

This is explained by Kaiyata and Nagesha to mean:*

> Even as the particles of fire in a flame momentarily arise and vanish and yet the flame and its light remain a continuity, so even in the words seemingly appearing and disappearing the continuity of knowledge (as the eternal Word-Principle in God) remains unaffected.

---

* These quotations here are repeated (though they occur before) intentionally, with a slightly changed translation.

Elsewhere, Patanjali discusses the *desiderative* formations in grammar (e.g., he desires to go: *jigamishati).* He traces this to the Will in Brahman,

> *sarvasya va chetanavattvat*
> for, all entities possess consciousness.
>
> *Mahabhashya III.1.1*

This is to show how the philosophers of language thought the words to be closely associated with the universal consciousness. Kaiyata says:

> "This is with a view to the non-duality of all self."

What these philosophers of language sought to do was to make every word of even a spoken language a vehicle for God-consciousness. They reiterated the principle that not only are the mantras handed down to us as revealed word, sacred and eternal

> *vedan no vaidikah shabdah*
> Patanjali's *Mahabhashya I.1.1*

but that

> *yah shastra-purvakam shabdan*
> *prayunkte so'bhyudayena yujyate.*
>
> *Ibid.*

> He who uses the secular words in accordance with
> the sacred tradition gains grace in life.

What does all this have to do with mantras? The answer, a summary of the above discussion, is in the Yoga and Tantra traditions described in the following principles of practice:

1. The mantras are the unalterable, permanent Word in God-Consciousness, vibrant in every living self.
2. A seeker must find the unity of all his verbal communication with the eternal Word-Principle through concentration on the mantra. This unity is real; all transient diversities of words, significations (i.e., meanings) and their relationships with the objects signified—all exist also at a deeper level of eternal unity.

> "from which they arise, in which they are
> supported, into which they merge"
> *Chhandogya Upanishad III.14.1*

I advise the reader to contemplate the above two principles and then review the discussion of the philosophy of language above. From there we continue again. We have not yet discussed the process by which the eternal word becomes manifest in these two forms:

> the revealed word, mantra or the scriptural text;
> and the diverse secular words.

A corollary to that discussion will also be:

> how to merge the secular words and the diversified
> consciousness into their transcendental origin.

As the process of *sphota* (bursting forth) occurs, a revealed word goes through the four states, that is, *para* etc., and the living and conscious energies within a seer come to special focus. From different concentrations of energy at different levels of personality, such as the *chakras,* various syllables burst forth into the mind. Of course, in the reverse process of meditation, learning to go deep into one's origins, the mental concentration on a mantra leads to a reawakening of relevant energies. It is thus that different syllables and letters are placed in various categories. For example we read in a Tantric text:

> The letters *a* and *ha* are the Lord and His consort,
> the Shakti (potentia)
> Void of form, embracing each other;
> Their nature is, respectively, vibration and
> illumination—
> This is Brahman as taught in the Upanishads
> *Varivasya-rahasya II.69*

The letters *a* and *ha* in the Sanskrit alphabet, equivalent to *alpha* and *omega,* with the addition of *M* representing *prana* and silence, comprise *aham, I,* the entire divine consciousness

> as the first person pronoun of the universe, and the
> total consciousness in a sentient person.

But of course, if the word *aham* occurs in a mantra, the mere translation "I" will not suffice; it will, however, mislead one to think of the little ego "I".

Just as the divine energy in the universe divides itself to become the cosmic male and the female, so the alphabet is divided into two. All the vowels are feminine, all the consonants masculine. Why are the vowels feminine? Because

> *svayam rajante.*
> They illuminate themselves.

The vowels are emitted from within when the conscious energy moves the *prana* in such a way that the breath subdivides into vowels. The vowels require no assistance from any other letter in order to be articulated. Such is the nature of feminine energy anywhere. It moves others but is itself moved by no other. The vowels support, help, the articulation of consonants but do not need their support. It is interesting to note that in at least the Indo-European languages, which are all related to Sanskrit, vowel sounds dominate over the consonants, thereby softening them, in the names for women. All vowels are variations on the primary vowel *a*. According to Ahirbudhnya-samhita:

a

i

u

ṛ

ḷ

e

o

these seven vowels represent the solar rays of consciousness.

ā

ī

ū

ṝ

ḷ

ai

au

these seven, *some of them not found in articulated language,* represent the lunar rays of consciousness.

> The sun leads the day moving by *Pingala* (the
> right energy channel) with its vowels.
> The moon creates the night moving by *Ida* (the
> left energy channel) with its own vowels.
> *Para,* the Lord's absolute, hidden
> brilliant power *(shakti)*

> moves by *Sushumna* (the central energy channel),
> extending the Word-God.
>
> *Ahirbudhnya XVI. 77-79*

Even though the terminology of these verses may seem mysterious to the noninitiate, the relationship between the science of language and mantras on one hand, and the science of breath on the other, is so close that the latter is called *svara-vidya*, the science of vowels. The authors of Tantras have gone into great detail to describe the revelation and arising of each possible syllable from various internal energies but it is impossible to explain even the beginnings of the process here. Take, for example, the following description, paraphrased from Abhinavagupta, the great polymath, yogi and master of Tantra in the eleventh century Kashmir.

> The Supreme dot, *bindu*, the transcendental point of God's self-luminosity has two emissions, the sounds *a* and *m; m* is the inward-closing, *a* is the outward-opening. When coming to diversification in the phenomenal world, its first emission, representing awareness of the creative power, becomes the sound *h*, divided into three types: the semivowel *h*, the emission of *h* from the heart (as the *nada* of *anahata-chakra*) and the sound *h* from the throat. Through the touch of the transcendental consciousness let the ear, throat and lips become one—and let the mind too become unified. This is the secret of the concentration on letters (of the mantras).
>
> *Tantrasara V.*

The text goes on to say that the experience of colors during meditation also arises as the letters of the mantra touch their natural origins in consciousness.

> The *a* and *h* represent the Lord and his feminine power, ever in their biunity. The sound *ā*,

when expressive of bliss, becomes the long *ā;* expressing the will to create becomes *i;* ruling over the creation it is the long *ī* (pronounced *ee*) (and so on, through all the letters of the alphabet).
Abhinavagupta's *Tantraloka, III*

The touch of the vibration of consciousness is not related to time, but the letters, dependent on time, are expressive of it. We would like to reproduce here the philosophical explanation of the mantra-ized letters of the Sanskrit alphabet from a brochure "On the Sharada Alphabet" by Sir George Grierson, a pioneer in the research on the languages of India in the nineteenth century.

"(a)—the first element in the conception of the Uppermost Ego, perfect Egoity, essentially transcendental in nature.

"(aa or ā)—the sinking to rest in that same (perfect egoity), hence the power of joy consisting in the combination of two aa or ā's.

"(i)—the power of Will, styled Aghora, consisting of an instinct towards external self-manifestation amidst the union consisting of the Equilibrium of Shiva.

"(ī or ee)—the same when mistress (isitri) is, as it were, fallen to rest in the Self, hence composed of the combination of two ī or ee's.

"(u)—the power of thought in the form of an opening out (unmesha) of a universe, while there is in (the Power of) Will an instinct outwards.

"(ū or oo)—a condition revealing deficiency in the principle of Consciousness, owing to the excess of the object of thought, while this (Power of

Thought) is still undivided like (the image) of a town in a mirror.

"(ṛ r̄)—as the twofold Will reposing upon the realm of the Void, touches the luminous principle (tejas) by the agency of the Power of Thought, it reveals itself in the sound r like the lightning-flash and the lightning.

"(ḷ l̄)—when the same (Will) advances far in the realm of the Void, and owing to a certain deficiency of the Power of Thought assumes the form of wood and stone, it reveals itself in the same way as the lightning-flash and the lightning, by means of the sound l because of its solid nature; hence these things (wood, etc.) are similarly eternal, because they sink to rest solely in the self. The term "neuter" is applied because (the l and l) are unable to generate any other letter (bija, a mystical letter forming the essential part of the spell of a deity), owing to their lack of instinct outwards.

"(e pronounced "ey")—a triangular radical (bija) due to the predominance of the Uppermost whilst the Uppermost and Joy are proceeding in Will, (its triangular form being) because of the equilibrium of Will, Thought and Action.

"(ai)—a prolongation owing to greater (vocalic?) sound as a result of the extreme extension of the same two (the Uppermost, represented by *a* and Joy, represented by *o*) in Will (the letter i) and the Mistress (the i or ee).

"(o)—having the form of an extension of the Uppermost and Joy, due to the desire for manifestation outwards, in the Power or thought (when the latter is) in the condition in which the universe opens out into manifestation.

"(au)—as this is an extreme prolongation of the same (vowel au) it is a trident-radical letter (tris'ula-bija) because Will, Thought and Action are distinct in it.

"(aṁ)—a power-inspired intuition for the first time of the universe, so far (as it yet exists), as being the Bindu, because it consists of sensation.

"(aḥ)—an intuition of the predominance of Power in the above-mentioned Uppermost (when the latter is) in unbroken union with the Power of Joy, (so that the Uppermost and the Power of joy are intuited) as being in the form of Visarga."

We further quote Mukunda Ram Shastri who edited the major works in the Kashmir series of texts:

Likewise on the bases of the vowels the creation of the consonants from k to h is effected. The consonants of the k, ch, p, ṭ, and t Series, being serially the developed forms of a, i, u, ṛ, and ḷ are like them gutturals, palatals, labials, cerebrals and dentals respectively, y and śh are but developed forms of ch; r and ṣh of ṭ; l and s of t while v is the developed form of t and p combined; h is the development of Visarga. To sum up, the Universe is an aggregate of the Matrikas from a to h and may be traced to a as its source. In the end the mystery of the Universe finds its solution in the enigmatical joint letter ksh which is but a combination of k, the developed form of a, or the Anuttara, and sh, the developed form of Visarga or Shakti. In other words, it brings to light the inseparability or oneness of Shiva and Shakti.

The import of the Universe as referred to before forms the subject-matter of all the Shastras. A, the Anuttara which is the origin of the Matrkas, being combined with the penultimate vowel aṁ and the last consonant h, in order of a, h and ṁ (Anusvara), and forming the word Aham, is an epithet of Aghora, the Omniscient One and is regarded as the essence of Para Vak, i.e., the All-Transcending Word. The dawning of the form or vision of Bhairava or Parama Shiva on the mind in the course of meditation and thereby the clearing away of the impurities is the way to recognition of oneself as Parama Shiva.

To conclude, the individual self is identical with the Supreme Self and can attain to perfection by stability of meditation on the significance of the word Aham.

from *Introduction to Para Trimshika*

The text itself says that

"Whosoever understands these meanings, will attain the final fruition of the mantra—so says the Rudrayamala (an ancient) Tantra. By the practice of these one gains the siddhi (and even) the knowledge of all things"

Para Trimshika, verse 35

Other Tantric texts teach these factors specific to each letter, namely,

symbolic forms,
power,
planet,
sign of the zodiac,
star cluster,
element,
numerological value,
day, date and time

—and so forth.

In fact, the first letter of a name upon a child's birth is

determined according to these principles. An initiate's new name is often determined similarly. Furthermore, the yogis often consider all the astrological signs to be in the states of breath and do their predictions and life readings accordingly. The deepest aspect of this science deals with the place of the letters in the various *chakras* (centers of consciousness),

> where the vibration first appears and *para* becomes *pashyanti;*
> where *madhyama* converts the Vibration into sequential mental thought;
> where the mantras again merge into *pashyanti,* leading the mentation to transcendence.

The *chakras* of the letters, fifty in this system, are as follows:

All the letters in undifferentiated *para* state	thousand-petal lotus	crown of the head
Ha, kṣha	*Ajna chakra*	between eye-brows
a,ā, i, ī, u, ū r̥, r̥̄, ḷ, ḹ, e, ai, o, au, aṁ, aḥ	*vishuddha*	pit of the throat
ka, kha, ga, gha, ṅa, cha, chha, ja, jha, ña, ṭa, ṭha	*anahata*	heart

da, dha, na, ta	*manipura*	navel
tha, da, dha, na,		
pa, pha		
ba, bha, ma, ya	*svadhishthana*	genital
ra, la		
va, sha, sha, sa	*muladhara*	coccyx

There are even special dictionaries in the Tantra tradition that give meanings and synonyms of each letter of the alphabet.*

---

* For an understanding of the scientific reasons for the sequence and order of these letters, the reader is advised to request information about the author's cassette course on Sanskrit.

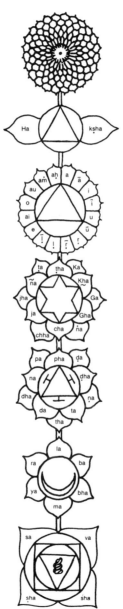

Part III

Mantra and You

9

The Character of the Mantra

No doubt, many readers are going to try to guess the "meaning" of their mantra merely on the basis of the scanty and incomplete information provided here. The mind simply does not want to move out of the grooves of a coarse association between a word and an external object at best and a mere translated sentence at worst. Unless the philosophy of language and syllables as we have explained above is understood, the practice of mantra will be misunderstood.

Ultimately it is not understanding but spiritual realization that matters, and it occurs only when the practice itself goes deep. The knowledge of the secret of mantras is received in the guru-disciple tradition, either as an experience imparted by the guru, or during one's meditations. In addition the personal instruction is passed on in *bhuta-lipi,* literally, script of the spirits, or script from the past. It is in fact a way of passing on the code concerning the mantras. Since it is impossible to give a complete detailed explanation about any mantra, and only someone initiated at a certain level can even comprehend the instruction, those specially entitled to the knowledge are taught in *bhuta-lipi* which is both

> a sign language going back to pre-Vedic times, and
> a system of code-words in which the detailed knowl-
> edge is passed on in a very condensed or oblique
> form, understood only by the initiate of that level.

Some of this code is so universal that the key to the symbols and scripts of many ancient civilizations can only be discovered by understanding this code. For example, take the choice of color in an ancient mural, equate it with the particular syllable asociated with that color, and you have a message! But the purpose of this work is limited to convey only what would be helpful to an initiate in the modern daily life. We do not pursue knowledge as information merely to satisfy a curiosity.

Is it then necessary that one should laboriously learn the Sanskrit language in order to understand the mantra? Further-more, in what way can we differentiate the revealed nature of Sanskrit from the similar claims made by Hebrew of the Old Testament, Arabic of the Holy Quran, or even Latin? Let us attempt to answer these questions.

The Sufi tradition that shares much with Yoga and Vedanta, wears the external garb of Quranic Islam while remaining above doctrinaire religions, and bases its teaching on direct experience. It developed in the countries of Central Asia (now under Russian occupation) which were centers of the Yoga and Buddhist learning before the take-over by Islam. It is interesting to note that some of the central chants of the Sufi tradition are similar to those of Tibet, for example the deep *Hum* or *Ho* in the *Allaho,* reverberated from the heart center. There are secrets within the Quran that are not understood by the commentators. For example, many of the books, *surais,* of the Quran begin with an utterance الم , that is *alef* (A), *laam* (L), *meem* (M), a word that cannot be pronounced properly without the linguistic elision of *laam* (L). The complete sound produced is similar to *Om*. Even though the translators of the Quran say that *ALM* means:

I have heard your prayer,

those in the know further state:

This is one of the merely exoteric, human-level translations provided by past commentators. It was in actuality a secret between God and the Prophet.

Maulana Hasan Nizami's Commentary,
Delhi, Hijri 1347 (1928 A.D.)

In other words the Prophet Mohammed kept this secret to himself, and used it as a "mantra" to go into the state where his consciousness responded to the revelation, *ilhaam,* being given. We also read

O Prophet, the very one who revealed the past books has given you this revelation and confirms these books that came down from heaven in the past.

Quran Sharif, surai Ali-imraan.
Commentary by Hasan Nizami.

In other words, the tradition of the Sufis cannot be seen as separate from the entire revelatory experience of humankind. The method of finding deeper meanings behind syllabic sounds is followed among the Sufis as it is among the students of Kabbalah. It is therefore to be concluded that so far as the method of unveiling a sacred utterance through experiential understanding is concerned, the traditions of Yoga, Sufism and Kabbalah all agree.

The uniqueness of Sanskrit, however, lies in the fact that its alphabet is the most complete, having 48 to 65 sounds

depending on the system used and the purpose of their analysis
or application. It is the most ancient and complete alphabet. It
is the first and last one devised and analayzed scientifically, with
all sounds placed in categories of articulatory method and
pattern. The word for education in Sanskrit, *shiksha,* simply
means *phonetics*—the science of sound. Another difference is
that even though the first letter of the semitic alphabets
(Hebrew and Arabic) is *aleph,* the system of vowels is
undeveloped. There are no independent letters for i, u, etc.,
except the signs of *zeer, zabr, pesh.* This leaves out the *shakti,*
the feminine energy, the *potentia,* the mother of the universe. A
language of mysticism based on masculine consonants is
lopsided, and will block the flow of energies rather than release
them. The articulation of consonants is impossible without the
release of a vowel sound to help it. Try to pronounce the sound
of the letter *k (kay* in the English alphabet) without *ay;* it will be
stuck in your throat. Try *B (Bee in English)* without the *ee* and
your lips will be stuck together! No wonder the modern
linguists call the consonants mutes! It is the release, the
exhalation of breath in the pronunciation of a vowel that helps
feminize the poor helpless consonant male! Unfortunately,
both the Sufi and the Kabbalah traditions analyze mystical
words and try to understand their power by taking into account
the consonants while treating the vowels as subsidiary; all roots
seem to be predominantly consonantal. Take any page of Idries
Shah's *The Sufis,* Anchor Books paperback, 1971, and the
above statement will be borne out. The Tantric *bindu* (from
which the English words *point* and *punctual* are derived) is
primarily a focus of *Shakti,* the feminine energy but compare
Idries Shah, page 422. The vowels of the Arabic word *Nuqtah,*
meaning a point, are omitted and the root shown is purely
consonants N Q T. The vowels of *Muhandis,* meaning a
geometrician, cease to exist; only M H N D S remains. In N K H L
(P. XV) the descent of energy would be impossible without the

shakti of mother vowels. You will similarly find: BRK, for Grace (p. 417), NSHR (p. 434), QLB (p. 438), and other words throughout. The same principle is followed in the Qabbalah, thus making the liberation of energy impossible, in spite of the vast riches of these traditions in other aspects. A large number of Hebrew and Arabic texts have become obfuscated because the scribes omitted or elided the vowel signs in many important lines. Because of this one cannot figure out whether QLB should be read as, QLB, Qilb, or Qulb! It has one adavntage—it keeps modern exoteric scholars employed! Another important point to remember is the vast richness of mantras in Sanskrit literature. According to *Svacchanda-Tantra (XI.55)* there are twenty million mantras. This author had to be able to explain the three-level meanings of twenty thousand mantras from the Vedas by the age of thirteen.

As to the Western languages ranging from Greek to English, there is no logical order to the alphabets. For example, there is no reason whatsoever why beta should follow alpha. They are so primitive that the sciences of linguistics and phonetics were virtually unknown until the Europeans conquered India and rediscovered the roots of their language in Sanskrit. If there was any tradition of mantras in pre-semitic* Europe, hardly any trace of it is left; a tragedy for humankind. The inner meanings of many words of Western languages can be understood only with the aid of Sanskrit, which in the words of the historian Will Durant:

> is one of the oldest in that "Indo-European" group
> of languages to which our own language belongs.
> *The Story of Civilization I.605*

Without the study of Sanskrit we cannot know that the words *wisdom* and *wit* along with German *Weise* and Latin *video* are

---

* Before the Judeo-Christian take-over in Europe.

derived from the Veda, the ancient collection of mantras. It also needs to be remembered that the mantras have always been written in a script of Sanskrit derivation in all countries from Bali in Indonesia to Lake Baikal in Siberia, i.e., wherever the knowledge of mantras spread. In China and Japan, where the concept of an alphabet did not develop beyond a rudimentary stage, the mantras were written in the *siddham* script, one of more than twenty forms of script in which Sanskrit has been recorded. When care is not taken in their transmission they become garbled. In Japan, for example, one often hears a mantra like

No-Mo Amidabutsu,

a garbled form of

Namo amitabhasya

which is a mantra of the Enlightened one as a Being of Immeasurable light. Similarly the Taoist priests of China, Korea, and related lands have corrupted many mantras because of the failure to transmit them correctly. In the original Sanskrit tradition the mantras have been handed down for nearly five thousand years orally, without the slightest change of annotation in a single vowel. Thus the effectiveness of the mantras as sound vibrations is maintained.

Having spoken so glowingly about the importance of Sanskrit in learning about mantras, we now need to put the meditator on the right track in a different direction. Here we can divide the mantras into three linguistic groups:

1. The mantras that are not in any human language at all.
2. The mantras which *appear* to be in Sanskrit and

even in other spoken languages. However, that is
not their reality, and

3. The Mantras that can indeed be translated by the
rules of a language but whose inner intent is known
differently to the yogis, and is realized by the
disciples after a long period of the practice of observances.

Let us take the three categories one by one. In the first
category fall the mantras known as *bija*-mantras, the seed-
words. The English word *bead*, as in prayer beads, is stated in
dictionaries to have been derived from Middle English *Bede*, a
prayer (related to many other Indo-European forms) and
Anglo-Saxon *Bedu* and *biddan*, to pray. The idiom *to count*,
(say or tell) the beads means: to say one's prayers with a rosary.
I suspect that the word may have its remote origin in Sanskrit
bija (pronounced *beeja*), a seed, not merely to indicate the seeds
of which the *mala* rosaries of India are made, but also to imply
that the prayer may contain seed words. The *bija*-mantras are
the most potent of all. They definitely belong to no language
and are not found in any dictionary. They have no gender and
no declensions. They are combinations of letters that represent
the relationship between the *kundalini* and the Supreme
Consciousness, and their specific rays. The highest of these
mantras is *Om*, on which alone volumes can be written. An
attempt to understand them intellectually will be futile; let us try
one anyway! The mantra *Hreem:*

H: Sun
R: fire
EE: feminine power in the universe; divine energy;
     shakti; divine mother
M: silence.

Here we have given the rough equivalents of the rays of

consciousness of this mantra. But, what does it really mean? What are the sun and the fire principles in the *kundalini?* This is a matter for experience. An intellectual mentation on the topic will only lead the mind astray from meditation. These words are definitely not Sanskrit.

The second category of mantras seem to be in Sanskrit or even in other spoken languages but the explanation given is often different from the meaning understood by lexicographers and grammarians. For example, let us take some Sanskrit words. *Namah* expresses homage, surrender, honoring, as the word is seen in *namaste,* a phrase for greeting. The Sanskrit-grammarians derive it from the verb root *nam,* to bend or to bow. The yogis have no respect for the rules set by grammarians. They say *namah* means 'not *mine'.* If a Sanskrit student gave this explanation in an examination he would surely fail. *Prana* is derived by the grammarians from:

> *pra* - forth
> *an* - to breathe (the verb root seen in anima, animal, animate) =
> *prana* - that which is breathed forth.

The yogis say:

> *pra* - first
> *na* - unit of energy.

Impossible in Sanskrit! Similarly, the word *guru* is related to the English great and gravity, from the verb root *gr,* to praise, to invoke, to utter. From where did the yogis get

> *gu* - darkness
> *ru* - to remove =
> *guru* - he who removes the darkness?

The earliest system of etymology, *Nirukta,* followed this very method to explain the Vedas. The grammarians refuted it, translators often ignored it and the modern scholars have rejected it. Yet it remains closer to the truth than all the researches combined.

This type of explanation takes these words from outside the realm of language. The concept

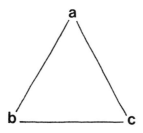

(abc) cannot be translated; cannot be found as a word in a dictionary. The words appearing to be those in a language, actually come from a system of communication used among the masters and their close disciples. This system is known as *sandha-bhasha,* the hidden language, often used to keep the secret tradition from the unqualified. Take a Sanskrit Tantra verse which is translated:

Eat beef daily and drink wine.

This is heresy to the cow-worshipping Hindus. The word for beef is *go-mamsa,* literally, cow's flesh. But from the Vedic times the words for *cow* also mean *speech.* The flesh of a cow is the tongue. Swallowing the tongue in *khechari mudra* and thereby tasting the nectar that flows from the celibate yogi's highest center is the purport of the passage, but the verse in *sandha-bhasha* is beyond the layman's power of understanding.

Another case in point is the phrase:

Let one enter the yoni to meditate.

It is understood as an admonition to enter *yoga-nidra, yoni* being an acronym in the *sandha-bhasha.*

Let one meditate in the presence of *shodashi,*

is yet another phrase we can examine. To an average reader of Sanskrit the last word means a beautiful maiden of sixteen. In *sandha-bhasha* it refers to mantras from sixteen vowel sounds which are regarded as feminine in principle! Similarly, where a mantra might appear to be a prostration to a deity, it actually represents a state of consciousness. Sometimes a Tantric might order a disciple to,

bring me a corpse tomorrow morning and I will worship Shiva on it.

The word for *corpse* is *shava* and the disciple is being advised to master the practices of the corpse posture in which the latter dies to his ego-being. By adding the seed-syllable *i*, the feminine principle of divine energy is awakened and *shava* the corpse becomes *Shiva* the deity! What other Shiva is there but the life-energy within ourselves? Now translate *namah shivaaya!* The experience alone is the meaning.

The third category of mantras follows the same system more elaborately because of the hidden depths in every word. Take the simple word *agni*, the fire, (Latin *ignis*), to which are related the English words *ignite* and *igneous. Agni* is the first word of the *Rig Veda* text and the hymn must be a praise to the fire-god. What else? But one erudite yogi explained this single word in 456 ways. One example is: the vowels are of water, the consonants are fiery. What are the fires of the *kundalini*, as compared to the sun in the *kundalini?* In one text we read

The *prana*-fires remain awake in this city.

The city is the body. Only by following prescribed observances would a disciple find out what fires within him a fire-mantra would invoke. To summarize, any translation provided for any mantra is incomplete and not the same as its meaning.

This brings us to another popular question: are not the mantras merely names of Hindu deities or prostrations to them? The question is based on two assumptions, one that Hindus are believers in polytheism, and two, the yogis are all Hindus. It should be understood that in all religions there is an element of polytheism. Christianity believes in a trinity, or tri-unity: *one* who is *three*fold. There are also Christian prayers to saints asking for many favors. In the monotheistic Islam there are also many figures like *Khijr*, the messenger of divine wisdom. Yet we read in the Sufi works:

> There are many numbers, but only One is counted.
> *The Secret Rose Garden*
> *of Shabistari, Pt. IV.*

Poets like Dante confirm that

> All numbers *ray* from unity.
> *Paradiso XV.55*

In their daily prayers the Hindus recite:

> As water fallen from the clouds
>   flowing in many streams and rivers
>   goes to one ocean,
> So the worship offered to all deities
>   reaches one God.

The yogis go further. They said: God is not one, cannot be one because one is a number, and God cannot be numbered. God is

Infinite. To understand the relationship of numbers with Infinity is to understand the relationship between all phenomena—worlds, atoms, souls, angels, deities, incarnations—and the Infinite being whose emanation they all are, in whom they dwell, and into whom they dissolve. To understand this more completely the author suggests a reading of his book titled *God.*

Since all phenomena are emanations of the Infinite, their names also are names of the same One. All Deities are His energies much as the Son and the Holy Ghost are said to be one with the One. *The vibrations of God's energies*—this phrase is synonymous with *the names of all deities.* In some yoga lineages the idea of giving and receiving a mantra is expressed as 'giving' or 'receiving' a name; not a new name for the disciple but a name of God as a mantra.

The Tantric texts have gone into great detail to demythologize the concept of many deities. One text, *Paratrimshika* (thirty verses on *para,* the transcendent Word) begins with

> *Devi uvacha:* the goddess said.

The great Tantric master and yogi of Kashmir, Abhinavagupta, spends fifty pages explaining the meaning of this simple statement. Briefly, he asks: when the power, *potentia, shakti* of the Lord is inseparable from Him, how is it possible for Her to speak, and to whom? It is said,

> the whole universe is His powers *(potentiae),*
> and He, the Great Lord is (omni) potent—
> the possessor of these powers.

Such being the case, there is no 'goddess' outside of Him. She, the Word, the Transcendental Speech dwelling within us, reveals His self to the little self within ourselves, and that experience is reported as 'the goddess said.' This is what all realized ones in many religions confirm. We read from the Sufis:

> Each creature has its being
> from the One Name,
> from which it comes forth,
> and to which it returns.
>
> *Shabistrai, pt X.*

No, then, the mantras are not names of Hindu gods. The Hindus, like many others before them and after them, have borrowed the sounds and often personalized them, declaring them to be names of God. The Light is One and the mantras are Its

nominal emanations

as the objects of the world are Its

phenomenal projections.

The Lawbook of Manu says,

> *atman,* the self is all the deities.
>
> *XII.124*

If you are devoted to a personal God you may use your mantra to invoke His presence, calling upon Her/ Him/ the Self of All, but know what Yajur Veda says:

> *Om, the space, the Brahman.*
>
> *XL.17.*

In that One Space there are no divisions of space and time and ultimately no names. "Nameless is the origin of things," says the

Book of Tao. If you are devoted to a particular name of God don't ever give it up, but remember that even that name is pronounced differently in many countries. Jesus bears the names Yesus, Yeshu, Yesu, Eesa, in different cultures and places. The English pronunciation 'Jesus' has come down as corrupted by many linguistic generations: Latin, Greek, Hebrew, Aramaic. By what name do the Christians in Arabic-speaking countries call God, and what is the word for God in the language of Malta, a Christian country? The answer to both is *Allah!* The divisions of names and languages are artificial and a meditator must not permit a conflict to enter his mind. He must reconcile and know that all prayer goes to God, leads the human consciousness to see, adore and touch the Light of the Divine Consciousness. If you belong to a religion or a church and receive a mantra within the yoga tradition, it should help you to concentrate on God within your church. Your moments of silence during worship must become more profound and your experience of the presence of God more real.

You may begin your meditation sessions with the prayers according to the teachings of your church. Slowly let the prayer cease to be verbal and let your whole heart and the mind pray silently, with an internal intensity. Gradually drift into your mantra and let it refine into a subtle vibration; let it lead you to the secret silent chamber. There, instead of speaking to God in a prayer, do shut up! Listen to God in silence.

These words have been addressed to those who wish to offer their person to a personal God. Theirs is the path of *bhakti*—devotion and surrender. Those who walk on the path of the Transpersonal and Transcendent have already surrendered; they place themselves at the disposal of the silent divine presence and patiently wait to be uplifted. They are not devotees, mystics, servants or worshippers of God, but merely *dasanudasa*—servants of the servants of God. They dwell in the silence of meditation, their mantra a bridge between mind and that pure Consciousness from which it emanated.

The bursting forth of the intuitive knowledge is not an isolated, infrequent, sporadic event. It is a part of that veiling and unveiling, creation and dissolution of the universe, which is the constant play of Divine forces. In the beginning of each cycle of creation a Being appears whose mental sparks are the very first wise men, the very first seers. If you read the ancient records of this tradition there are statements of who taught whom in a lineage of thousands of years, going back to that One of Whom the Yoga Sutras say:

> He is the Guru even of the ancient ones
> for he is never divided by time.
>
> *1.26*

In this aspect of Teacher, He is spoken of as *Hiranya-garbha,* the Golden Womb, or even the golden egg. All yogis trace their lineage of teaching to this one Being. From him emanates Manu, the personification of mantras. The most common Sanskrit word for human being is *manushya,* the offspring of Manu. Let us therefore look to the Lawbook of Manu, the first lawgiver, Chapter One.

5. It was all turned dark,
    not recognizable, without marks,
    unanalyzable, unknowable,
    as though asleep all over.
    (Compare Genesis I.2: *And the earth was without form; and darkness was upon the face of the deep.*)

6. Then the Self-Existent Being, the Lord,
    unmanifest, manifesting all
    these elements and so forth,
    with His power activated,
    appeared, the dispeller of darkness.

7.   He who is beyond the grasp of the senses
         Subtle, Unmanifest, Eternal,
      Who is one with all beings, beyond thought—
         the very One Himself shined forth.

8.   Intent on creating the various progenies
         from his own body,
         having meditated
      He first created the very (cosmic) waters
      and released (His) seed upon them.

9.   That became a golden egg
         with the splendor of a thousand suns.
      In that was born Brahma
         Himself the Creator,
         the Grandfather of all the worlds.
      (Compare Genesis 1.7: *And God made the firmament and
      divided the waters.*)

10.   The (cosmic) waters are called *Nara*
         for, they are the child of *Nara*—
         the cosmic Person, the Lord.
      Since He first dwelt upon them
         therefore He is called *Narayana.*
      (Compare Genesis 1.2: *And the Spirit of God brooded upon the
      face of the waters.*)

11.   That which is the Eternal, Unmanifest Cause,
         Comprising both being and non-being—
      created by That One the (cosmic) Person
      is called *Brahma* in the world.

12.   Having dwelt in that (golden) egg for a year
         that Lord, through the meditation
         of his own Self,
      divided that egg twofold.

32.   Dividing His body into two
         He became a male by one-half

and by the other half a female.
In her the Master created *Viraj*
(the Unitary principle of the universe of multiple phenomena).

33. Manu says:
Whom the Viraj Person created
after undertaking ascetic fervor—
know me to be that, O best of the learned,
as the maker of it all.

34. I, in turn, having gone through
very difficult ascetic observance
first of all created ten great seers,
prajapatis, fathers of beings;

35. Namely, Marichi, Atri, Angiras,
Pulastya, Pulaha, Kratu,
Prachetas, Vasishtha,
Bhrgu and Narada.

36. These, shining with profuse brilliance,
created seven other Manus,
deities, the shining ones, and
Godly seers of immeasurable power.
(The subsequent verses list other beings, elements, worlds and
species being created, together with their power, wisdom and
merit).

51. Having thus created me
and all of this world,
He whose stride is beyond thought
concealed Himself within Himself
pressing time with Time.

52. When that Shining One *(deva)* is awake
then this whole world remains active;
When He sleeps with (in) His Pacific Self,
then everything closes its eyes.

57. Thus with His wakefulness and sleep
    that immutable One
    brings to life all this
    moving and unmoving world
    as well as brings it to dissolution.

We have explained this scheme of creation in simpler
English in our book titled *God.* In cycle after cycle of the
creation of the universe

the Great Self stirs up the waters of matter,
upon which he casts the seed of His Will.

The Golden Egg, *Hiranyagarbha,* the cosmic Person,
the Holy Ghost, descends into the creation.

It divides into the male and female principles
of the universe, and
sends forth cosmic wise beings, shining ones, spirits
that direct worlds and the mortals,
descend as Manus who are the collective consciousness of
mantras,
producing individual minds of great seers
into whose minds their minds further descend.

These seers, rishis, founders of the yoga science
pass on this knowledge to less luminous minds,
to illuminte them, to link them to their conscious
Origin Who has concealed Himself within Himself.

In the words of Swami Rama, there is no evolution of
collective consciousness. The very first human was a seer who
knew this science of the lights of a thousand suns, was a shining
one, a m(p)atriarch in wisdom for the whole human race. (S)He
and all his/her companions, *prajapatis* (progenitors), Manus
(Mantra-minds), *rishis* (Seers) have passed on this knowledge
in an unbroken chain of grace, their minds linked to minds.

Those disciples who have been touched by the presence of the Masters of this lineage even in our age understand what is spoken of here. Many, however, surmise, guess and shake their heads in disbelief.

Those who are true to the tradition pay homage, not to the Guru personage, but to the spiritual Principle in which all seekers are linked to that One Who has concealed Himself within Himself and plays hide-and-seek within us who are His own divided selves. At the end of a cycle He gathers the selves into the Self and at the beginning of another cycle diversifies them again, sending into them the *sphota* of *para vak,* a burst of the Transcendental Word. The first book of mantras known as the Vedas, was introduced to America by Walt Whitman in his *Passage to India.*

> Passage to more than India!
> Are thy wings plumed indeed for such far flights?
> O Soul, voyagest thou indeed on Voyages like those?
> Disportest thou on waters such as those?
> Soundest below the Sanskrit and the Vedas?
> Then have thy bent unleash'd.

The first custodians of this knowledge are four seers:

Agni:	Fire
Vayu:	Air *(prana)*
Aditya:	Sun
Angiras:	The essence of Embers.

These are the titles given them at the beginning of each cycle of creation.

It is not that the knowledge is handed down once and for all. Great seers, whose intuitive vision is as sharp as that of a high-flying eagle *(shyeno bhutva),* are born throughout the times, continually refreshing the stream of knowledge. Knowledge never stays concealed long; it awaits the opening of the third eye anywhere and then shows itself. Thus the same mantras may be revealed again and again to different beings. The 'authorship' of each is attributed to the seer to whom it was last revealed.

A mantra from the Vedas is never recited without first stating its

> *seer,* to whom it was revealed, to whom our homage is due;
> *deific power* contained in it;
> *metre* of its composition;
> *accentuation*
>   or
> *annotation* of its recitation (like musical notations that have been passed in a mnemonic lineage, *amnaya,* for forty, fifty centuries).

A student is also taught its *viniyoga,* application in specific spiritual practices and observances. Those born in this tradition must also know the name of the seer or *rishi* to whom their lineage traces its origin. To be born in the lineage means to go through rigorous observances that begin before conception and continue throughout life. If the heart, mind and character is not pure, knowledge is withheld.

The mantras of the Vedas are not normally given widely in the Western world. Of approximately twenty thousand only two are taught to special disciples for specific purposes at certain times of their development. One of these, the most sacred and important of all the Vedic mantras, is known as

> *gayatri,* the protector of *pranas,* or the savior of one who recites it devotedly,
>   or
> *savitri,* daughter of the (spiritual) Sun.

Since accentuation, an all-important element in the Vedic mantras, can only be taught orally, we give here the shallowest-level translation of the basic skeleton of this mantra:

> In earth, sky and heaven
> We meditate upon the burning splendor
> of the Sun Divine
> Who may inspire our wisdom.

Since it was first revealed to the seer Vishvamitra, countless generations of seekers have learned it as their first and last mantra and have recited it daily. They have developed many ascetic observances around it. One may still find some devotee standing on one foot in the waters of the river Ganges, facing the rising sun at 4 a.m., with hands clasped, practicing daily until perhaps *ten million* recitations have been completed. For a beginner it might be only ten thousand repetitions. This mantra imparts all intuitive wisdom and expiates all *karma* for those seekers, with the capacity and strength to endure the burning of one's mental chaff.

The other Vedic mantra sometimes taught is the *mrtyun-jaya,* or death-conqueror. It heals, wards off the fangs of death, and vanquishes one's fear of death. On a shallow level it translates as follows:

> We sacrifice unto the one with three eyes,
> the fragrant one who increases nurture.
> Like a fruit from the vine
>   May I be liberated from death
>   and not from immortality.

There are actually four traditions of the mantras used and taught by the yogis:

is a combination of two basic yantra units:

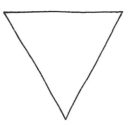

representing the descent of energy, and

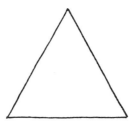

the ascent of energy.

Since the ascending and the descending energies meet in the heart center, it is the basic symbol of that *chakra.* There its ruling mantra is

although the teacher may assign some other special mantra for specific practice. The yantras have been called the visual forms of the mantras, or simply visual mantras which the mind is taught to visualize under a teacher's direction.

In the case of each Tantric mantra one needs to know its

rishi:	seer
devata:	deific power
chhandas:	metric composition, rhythm
svara:	accentuation, annotation
prayoga:	application in a special observance or for a specific purpose
bija:	seed, a fraction of itself or an associated mantra that contains the seed of its power
shakti:	a fraction of itself that expresses its power
kavacha:	armor, or
kilaka:	a stake, the recitation of which firmly prevents the mantra's power and mental concentration from being scattered away from the practitioner.
nyasa:	the process by which various sounds in the mantra are identified with the energy in particular limbs—

and numerous other aspects and processes of the mantra. A Tantric text says:

> these are all but the external aspects of the practice
> well-known to the ordinary people.
> Very difficult to find is the internal practice
> which (alone) should be respected by
> those who are turned inward.
>
> *Varivasya II. 161, 162.*

For this reason the yogi may not always find it necessary to lead the disciple through the externalized practice of all these aspects of his or her mantra. He may instead choose to teach or convey the internal experience of breath, *prana* and the *kundalini*. Without this particular category of mantras it is not possible to open the *kundalini*. Any *kundalini* experimentation *without* the control of these mantras is dangerous and will lead to serious consequences.

The fourth category of the source of mantras is the *Apta*. The word has two meanings: 'those found', and, the 'wise and noble'. The *Apta* mantras are not found in any text. One finds them by serving the wise and noble teachers in whose mental custody these mantras have remained and who themselves had originally found them through similar service to elders and sages. The *Apta* mantras fill the gaps in the otherwise detailed knowledge of yoga. An example of an *Apta* mantra can be seen in Swami Rama's story entitled, 'A mantra for bees' in his *Living with the Himalayan Masters* III.4. Sometimes when Swamiji has taught me a mantra, the Sanskrit scholar's ego in me has objected to its inaccurate Sanskrit grammar or diction. His response is that mantras do not go by the rules of any language. "This is the way the sound is. This is an *Apta* mantra. Accept it as it is given."

The process of revelation does not transpire only in the beginning of the cycle of creation, but continues from time to time. Furthermore, the entire revelation of the Vedas, the wisdom of the mantras and sciences, may not occur all at once. Different individual seers are vessels fit for serving as conduits of different types of knowledge and segments thereof. So the Vedas, the Puranas, the Tantras, as well as the *Apta* mantras are revealed at different times, thus creating a history of the sacred literature. The revelation itself is not historical. The chronology is unimportant. It is its eternity that is important. Its relationship with each individual forms the basic value system and we remain indebted to the long line of teachers through whom this revelation comes to us. Our relationship with this lineage of gurus is through the process of initiation, which is a different form of revelation.

10

Initiation and the Initiator

A higher mind reveals truth to a less developed mind. The cosmic mind of God reveals, transfers truth into the minds of individual seers. Similarly, those who have reached a certain state of development in their spiritual search, also become qualified vessels to receive a part of the revelation. The mind of the guru or a qualified initiator, transfers a particle of its knowledge into the mind of the initiate. This is called initiation. It must not be confused with a ritual ceremony or religious sacrament. On the other hand, it may be regarded as a spiritual sacrament confined to no particular religion. The initiation begins the process of sanctifying the initiate by placing in his mind a seed that might grow over a period of time if irrigated and nourished through regular practice and related disciplines. It must be understood that the process of initiation is not merely transferring information vocally from one conscious mind to another. It is not learning a language by memorizing words, or a science by memorizing formulas. It is a process of direct transfer of mental energy from one mind to another. It is said in the Vedas that this knowledge:

was the first semen of the Lord's mind.
The inspired wise ones found a friend of the
existent within the non-existent.
They found this wisdom by searching in the
heart of consciousness.
                                        Rig Veda X.129.

To have a mantra is to find a guide in what appears to be non-existent transcendental being, as though a friend for the realm of relativity. The process of initiation is like an impregnation. An impregnation of mind. It is as though a seed is emitted from the higher mind and is implanted into a weaker mind, there to gather strength and to give strength from within. It is the transmission of a minute particle of higher energy through the channel called the guru. In the ancient times the initiate was required to stay in the guru's ashram for at least three days and three nights, fasting in silence, dwelling alone in a hut, not answering if his name was called by any other but the guru. It was as though he was in the guru's womb for three days and three nights. The hymn on celibacy says:

the guru bringing the god-wandering celibate
unto himself, takes him into his womb.
He bears him in his womb for three nights.
All the gods gather around to look at him.
                                        Atharva Veda XI. 3.

This was meant to be a rebirth, a new beginning. It was the burning of oneself in a fire, to be born again, the mind carefully prepared. In modern times also there are many traditions in which a candidate for mantra initiation is chosen with great care. However, in the tradition of the Himalayan Institute the power of the guru itself has taken the responsibility for preparing the initiate, so the seed is being scattered widely, even if some fall by the wayside.

This answers the question as to whether it is appropriate

to read a book and select a mantra on one's own. Those who advocate such a course are simply responding to that ego which has not learned the practice of meekness and humility. The use of a self-chosen mantra will be a mechanical repetition, but will not touch those depths where the hidden *samskaras* carry on their undersea commotions.

The mantra imparted by a qualified guru may even remain in one's consciousness from incarnation to incarnation. Swami Rama recounts in *Living with the Himalayan Masters* that when his guru gave him his mantra at the age of three, he said to his gurudeva, "But I have been practicing this mantra already!" In such cases the guru in this life is serving only as a vehicle of encouraging reminiscences. According to Socrates' *Republic*, all knowledge is reminiscence of what was already within one's consciousness. This is even more true in the case of mantra. Since the mantra is merely the vocalization of the consciousness energy from within, the imparted vocalized mantra is the vehicle of that reminiscence which encourages the arousal of the response from within the initiate. Many times the initiate does not realize how fortunate he is to receive a mantra from a qualified guru. I recall many years ago an incident as follows:

> I sat receiving some instructions from my guru,
> H.H. Swami Rama. In the middle of the conversa-
> tion he asked me, "Are you doing your mantra?" I
> said, "Yes, indeed." "Which mantra are you doing?"
> he asked. "Oh, the same one that you gave me at the
> initiation," I replied. "Well, recite it," he com-
> manded. I had already done this mantra many
> million times in my mind while walking, talking,
> and even sleeping, but at this moment my mind was
> completely blank. I sat rubbing my forehead,
> completely embarrassed. There was no mantra in
> the mind—I could not remember it. I was extreme-
> ly uncomfortable and looked at my guru as he sat

impassively looking back at me. After I had rubbed
my head for two or three minutes trying to
remember my mantra, he said to me, "No, you
cannot. If I choose it to be so in my presence you
cannot remember your mantra. All right, now
remember it. What is your mantra?" And suddenly
my mantra was there!

This is to demonstrate that the mantra is not mine to hold, not a
bit of information that is controlled from the conscious mind. It
is indeed a transmission from the line of gurus. In the beginning
phase of teaching meditation under Swamiji's guidance, I went
through a short period when I would *struggle* a little at the time
of initiation, wondering whether or not I was giving the right
mantra. Sometimes it happened that as soon as I finished a
particular session of five or six initiations, the phone would
ring. It was Swamiji calling to reprimand me.

"Who do you think you are? Why do you think that
you are giving a mantra? Is it within your power?
Why do you not simply surrender? Why do you
struggle so much? Why do you not let it come
entirely on its own when I am here helping you and
guiding you?"

After a while I simply abandoned the struggle and let the guru's
consciousness guide me. There have been times though, when I
have given a mantra and in looking at it after a day or two, have
felt surprise: "Why did I give this mantra to such-and-such an
individual? It does not seem to make sense. Maybe I should
change it." Later I ask Swamiji, "I gave such-and-such a mantra
to so-and-so, but it doesn't seem right to my conscious mind!"
And he said:

"When you gave the mantra, you were a divine
being. Now you are thinking of it in human

consciousness. Let the divine being do what it must
do and you, the mere human, not interfere with it.
Whatever mantra came at that time was not yours
and is not yours to change."

It is because of the authenticity of such a transmission that
many initiates in the tradition of the Himalayan masters find
that the mantra arises in the mind without being invoked. One
may wake up at night and find that the mantra has awakened
him. It arises in the mind of its own accord while the person is
driving, walking, or even when in the arms of his or her loved
one. This is not the doing of a mere human consciousness but
rather the energy of pure ever-present consciousness being
gradually awakened into the mind of the initiate from a layer of
his being that is deeper than the conscious mind and *purer* than
his subconscious or unconscious mind. When the mantra is
given by a qualified initiator it will certainly have its effect. The
problem is to find a qualified initiator.

U nfortunately there are initiators in certain schools who
have not even mastered the correct pronunciation, not to
mention accentuation and annotation of the mantra. People
are giving mantras from their notebooks or in response to a
questionnaire, as though the mantra could be given as the result
of an aptitude test based on someone's age, sex, education or
profession! A would-be initiate must be wary of such initiators
and of the schools they belong to, because the mantra given by
an unqualified teacher can later on lead to the problems in the
prana field as well as in the *kundalini* force. Many times
initiates practicing within the tradition of such schools find
themselves getting uncomfortable or ill without being able to
define their illness. This is the nature of *prana* disorder or the
disturbances of the *kundalini* which neither they themselves nor
their initiators are able to control or channel properly.

When you are looking for an initiator, always try to

authenticate his tradition. From whom has he studied? Can he trace his lineage to a Himalayan master? What proof has he of being authorized by such a master to be an initiator? It is not through the human effort that the initiation occurs, but rather as an act of compassionate grace. Once again, it is not the initiator who initiates. It is always the guru who initiates. Many people become emotionally attached to their initiators as though the latter himself were the guru. At times these initiators even consciously, directly or indirectly, encourage such emotional attachment and dependence and thereby become themselves impure of mind. It must be remembered that the mantra does not come from the initiator no matter how qualified he is. If the thought arises in his mind that 'I am an initiator initiating this person,' the guru's spirit no longer works through him. The word 'I' is the ego-builder. The true aim of any serious seeker on the path of Yoga is to be able to forget the first person pronoun because this word alone, of the entire human language, is the barrier between the purity of transcendental consciousness and the highest potential of the individual consciousness. The qualified initiator is he who can forget this 'I' and surrender his being to the guru's spirit that works through him. For the same reason the would-be initiate preferring one particular initiator within the same guru tradition is irrelevant. Someone you are attracted to as your personal teacher ceases to be a person when he begins to be a teacher or an initiator. Even those teachers of Yoga who are not initiators but who have a guru of the Himalayan lineage, have found that when they sit down to teach their individual fears and complexes cease, and some other force flows out through them, not from them. Many times in the middle of the teaching, a student asks a question that the teacher himself has been struggling with. Suddenly the answer arises from an unknown source within. The process of initiation on the part of the initiator's mind is more or less the same except that it is more concentrated. The Yoga Sutra

(IV.4) says that a yogi may use sparks of his mind to create other beings working under the direction and guidance of his original mind. One need not look for some suspicious-looking being who appears to be a cloned copy of the guru's physical body! The ability to work through other minds as though they were his own is the mark of a true guru. But this power comes only when total obedience to the law of benevolence has been perfected. Wherever there is the slightest touch of personal ego and enjoyment of individual power, the manifestations of transcendental principles cease. To think that a real guru could ever wish for any personal desire, benefit or power, is to accuse Christ of serving his self-interest. Only a Christ-like being is the real guru, but the guru himself does not say "I am the initiator." He says,

> I work on behalf of my guru.

All the way up the line all the gurus make the same statement until we come to That One of whom it is said:

> His praises are sung by the most ancient seers
> as well as by the new ones.
> May he bring the shining ones to us.
>
> *Rig Veda I.1.2.*

It is the same Ishvara, lord of the universe, who is

> The guru of even the most ancient ones
> for in him there is no interruption of time.
>
> *Yoga Sutras I.26*

An initiator, as any Yoga teacher, is moved by two motivations or sentiments:

> indebtedness and gratitude,
> compassion.

He is infinitely indebted and feels deep gratitude for the lineage of the gurus on whose behalf he works. There is no way he can pay his debt to his own guides and teachers who have removed the blindfold of darkness from his eyes and shown him the path on which he may walk for many incarnations until he reaches the goal of enlightenment. Unless one pays the debt back in some way, one is guilty of ingratitude and his knowledge shall not prosper. What material goods are equal in value to the intuitive knowledge flashing from the superconscious, which can be given to settle this debt? There are none. The only way one may reduce the indebtedness is by giving to others what one has received. Those who are within the tradition often have no other choice. They are impelled for no conscious reason at all.

> *Brahmanena nishkarano dharmah.*
> A child of God performs the right acts for no
> reason whatsoever.
>   Patanjali's *Mahabhashya I.1.1.*

The inclination to teach and impart the wisdom of the tradition becomes a natural part of life. It is not a profession but a calling from within. Something other than one's self is impelling the initiator to serve the guru by sharing with others a small particle of the knowledge received.

The other motivation is compassion. There is much suffering in the world. A Yoga teacher or an initiator is not an enlightened being—very far from it. He is not yet a guru or a master. He too has his own suffering, his own sorrow somewhat reduced, somewhat under his own control. Whatever his state before entering the path, he is now able to take his own suffering in hand and give it a new direction through service. But there is yet much suffering in the world in varying degrees. It is not out of pity that he acts but out of compassion. In pity we cry when someone else cries. In compassion we replace someone's cries with our own laughter of joy. It is out of compassion for the suffering of others that he is required by the guru tradition to impart a moment of peace and to serve as a channel of divine knowledge as though bringing light to a chamber where someone had stumbled in the dark.

As one becomes confirmed in these attitudes and attains efficiency and perfection in them, his teaching becomes more and more efficacious, more and more successful. The test of an initiator is his purity with regard to these two attitudes. He must have no material expectation from his student other than what serves to enhance his mission of service. He must not let the student become dependent on him. The initiator must do what is necessary to make the initiate emotionally strong, to encourage commitment in his relationships, and confrontation of conflicts and difficulties. He must try to bring harmony into the life of the initiate and constantly instruct him to lead a strong family life, for if one does not pay one's debts to human relationships, he certainly cannot pay his debts to the divine ones. One who has not served one's own parents will not serve the teacher's mission for long. There must not arise in the initiator's mind a sexual thought towards the students of the opposite sex. They must be treated as mothers, sisters, daughters; as fathers, brothers, sons.

Many people are confused as to their relationship with the teachers and initiators. In the modern society we know of relationship with the parents, school teachers and, to a lesser degree, with our priests. Towards each of these, many people harbor certain resentments. They drop out of these relationships and then seek a "spiritual relationship." However, there are no models available in the modern society for a spiritual relationship. It often becomes a substitute for the other relationships one has missed. In the beginning the students become very dependent on their teachers and call that a spiritual devotion. The teacher's own ego also glows with all the attention showered upon him. This is not only unhealthy for both the teacher and the taught, it is conducive only to strengthening the values of ego, especially in the teacher, which then blocks his own further spiritual progress. Many times teachers who have gathered a certain number of adoring students around them, begin to think of themselves as equal to the guru and create separate followings. This has happened in the case of many great masters including Christ in whose name the churches pretend to serve. In the lifetime of the Buddha there is the example of Devadatta who formed a separate band of monks and created no end of trouble for his erstwhile master. Many times such teachers are not even aware that it is ego playing tricks on them, for they consider themselves very refined and purified. 'Don't all these students love me, adore me? It must be because I'm so pure, so wonderful.' Two things happen as a result of this:

1) There being no guide to control the processes of ego, these teachers soon fall into the traps of the subtle psychic and astral worlds. These realms are very exciting but easily lead seekers away from the actual path of pure realization. Just because you are occasionally able to hear your hunches or predict some little future event, does not make you into a master. You are not a master of the *kundalini* just because a light or two shines out in your meditation or some sensation is felt in the base of the spine. But the teacher wants to believe in his own assumed perfection especially in regard to his ability to guide the students. Quite often such teachers even invent experiences they have not had. They make up accounts of these experiences by reading other people's books or through mere speculation. The ego, however, invariably continues to take its toll. A certain expectation builds up. The teacher wants the students' surrender when he himself has not surrendered to a higher guide.

2) The students, on the other hand, have their own

expectations based on dependencies. Nowadays people often think that because they have grown independent of their parents and all their school teachers, they are truly *independent*. But the human needs remain, and the teacher often becomes a father or mother figure. Now each student demands a thousand hours of the teacher's time. And the moment the teacher is not able to give it or does something that is just slightly unpleasant to the student, all the rebellion the student had pent up towards his own parent figures and school teachers comes to the front and the teacher is discarded. The student moves on to repeat the same type of emotional episodes from teacher to teacher and from school to school.

An initiator's relationship with his students must be absolutely free of all expectation. Whatever help he desires from the student should be in the way of fulfilling an unselfish and pure mission. Everything must be directly or indirectly related to that. Secondly, he must not present himself as greater than he is. He must always issue a disclaimer as regards his own power, capacity, knowledge, wisdom or spiritual experience. His school must not become a club where people come to gossip about their spiritual experiences. He must diligently work for the benefit of his students so that he continues to guide them on the path of more and more purification. He must also prepare his students to reach a point where he can invoke the guru's blessing and grace on them, bringing his select students to the attention of the guru when they are qualified. When he has taught all he can and can lead them no further, he must pass them on to the guru. He must not draw the guru's attention to the students to waste the guru's time where he himself can be helpful. He must discourage any dependency on the part of his students even though they do not have a role model other than that of the parent or the school teacher. He must create a fresh model. The relationship with the guru or with the Yoga teacher is not like the relationship with the parent or the school teacher, because it is purely a spiritual relationship. Even though many mantras are imparted for both spiritual as well as therapeutic reasons it is not a substitute for a college course nor a more economical way of obtaining therapy.

The initiator is responsible for guiding his student for the rest of his life as long as the initiate retains the relationship from his end. The initiator or the Yoga teacher is what the Buddha called a

kalyana-mitra
a noble friend.

His task is: to keep reminding his friend of the path that lies ahead; to criticize him whenever he wavers from the path; to advise him when his personal behavior, thoughts, words and acts, emotions and relationships are not conducive to spiritual progress and purification; to encourage practice of the *yamas* and *niyamas;* to observe the disciplines; and to maintain the practice of meditation. It is the duty of the teacher and the initiator to constantly encourage the student to practice the four right attitudes in order to overcome the nine impediments and their five companions. Socrates was teaching his students even after he had drunk hemlock. The Buddha's chief disciple, Ananda, tried to prevent an inquirer from entering the Buddha's presence as the latter lay on his death bed. When the Buddha heard the conversation, he asked Ananda to let the inquirer come in and ask his questions. Even up to the last moment the Buddha taught. Even up to the last moment Christ invoked God's forgiveness on those who had erred in ignorance. Great masters teach even through their death. A Yoga teacher and especially an initiator is at the disposal of his students in spite of any physical discomforts. He should be able to teach even as he lies on his death bed. Such is his relationship with the initiate. In an era where relationships are being considered temporary experiences that one drops in and drops out of, it is difficult to understand this type of permanency. The path of enlightenment is not of temporary fads. It is a pursuit of the eternal.

Once you have embraced this path, you belong to the lineage of the masters of the Himalayas. There should then remain no further doubt about the efficacy of your mantra or about the initiator's lineage, because he is not working on his own behalf. There should be no conflict as to the choice between two initiators of the same lineage because they are not acting in an individual capacity as individual names.

11

Levels of Initiation

How does the initiator know which mantra to give? This question is to be answered in several different ways. Every person belongs to a specific personality type and there are mantras for the particular personality types. The great teachers of ancient India have written as well as taught orally in unwritten tradition the science of *purusha-pariksha*—the study of personality types. There is nothing in the physical body that is not a projection of the subtle body. All your *samskaras* (accumulations) of past lives, all the thoughts that you have thought during this life, all the acts committed or performed, all your predispositions, propensities, tendencies, inclinations and accumulated experiences, are made physical in your body and personality. That slight tilt of the head; that wrinkle on one side of the face hardly visible to the unobservant; the way you enter a room; how you sit, smile, laugh, speak, hesitate or go dashing about; your entire bearing with its subtle tones, undertones and overtones, form a single complete whole constituting your personality type. An observant and sensitive meditator looks with concentration, and, as it were, the constitution of your subtle body is on the screen of his mind. Quite often the would-be initiates say, "You hardly know my name. How can you determine what mantra to give me?" But remember that your name is not you. Your name is an artificial imposition on you as we have said earlier. When you were born, you did not come out of the mother's womb and say, "Hi, Mother, I am Mary." Your association with your name was formed later. It is what your mind is and how it reflects in your person that constitutes the real you. A perceptive teacher may forget your name but never forgets you, the picture that is present to his mind. The science of *purusha-pariksha* is an extremely detailed one. Another name for it is the science of Samudra. One of the earliest founders of the science, whose original name is unknown, called himself Samudra—most probably a pen name. The word itself means "he who is master of the *mudras*" or the gestures of body language. What is known as palmistry in the West today, is merely a small chapter in the book of *Samudra*—the chapter dealing with the hands. But the book goes on in detail to describe every limb and the balance of the entire body system by which a teacher may determine the mental status of an individual student. For example, *Visuddhi-Magga,* the most important primer of the Southern school of Buddhist meditation, says that a teacher should not admit a student, the arch of whose foot does not touch the ground as he stands. Such a person is extremely sensuous and will not take to disciplines. This may or may not be so, but the important point is that the Yoga science has developed a study of personality types and appropriately matched mantras of which a teacher must be thoroughly knowledgeable and proficient.

More important than the initiate's personality type, however, is the purity of surrender in the mind of the initiator at the time of giving the initiation. A good teacher of meditation must be able to separate the flashes of intuition from those of the subconscious mind. Unfortunately, an average human being is so completely in slavery to the subconscious mind that he will mistake many thoughts as intuitive or spiritual when they are actually just so much scum floating up from the depths of subconscious swamps. We often hear beginning meditators say, "This thought came to me in my meditation! This must be the guidance I have received from God or Guru!" Beware of such thoughts. Quite often people end up doing silly things thinking them to be guidance received from the Superconscious.

At the moment of transmission of initiation, an initiator must be free of this tyranny of the subconscious. He must not determine an individual's mantra on the basis of associations he has with his own past preferences, even though in his ordinary life he may continue to be an individual in bondage—which all of us are until we reach the final degree of enlightenment. The process of initiation itself is so sacred that it must be undertaken with utmost unselfishness and purity, a sincerity both towards the lineage of the guru tradition as well as deepest unselfish love and compassion towards the student whom the initiator serves on behalf of the guru lineage. All personal biases and prejudices must be set aside. The initiator must be unaware of the race, nationality, caste, religion or sex of the initiate. He should forget the existence of his own body completely and become merely a vehicle of the guru.

In some schools of Yoga a particular practiced art is called *guru-bhava.* This practice consists of a student imagining himself to be the image of the guru. At times one looks in the mirror and expects to see the face of the guru and is surprised to see his own old, individual face. When one has achieved mastery of this practice, all the knowledge of the guru flows easily through him. At least at the moment of initiation this *guru-bhava* must be complete—

evam me sutam

so have I heard from the elders.

The theory of mantra initiation is expounded in detail in the Kashmir School of Tantra known as the philosophy of vibration, or *Spanda.* The school was founded in early ninth century by the great Master Vasugupta who was directed in a dream to go to a certain mountain rock in Kashmir to find the seventy-six aphorisms, the Shiva-sutras, inscribed on the rock. The Sutras are divided into three sections dealing with the three ways of initiation as well as the three levels of mantra experience. These three *upayas* are called:

anava: to a being of limited awareness who
(physical)   identifies the self with an atomic, physi-
              cal, personalty;

shakta: to one in whom *shakti,* the spiritual
(psychic)   energy is awakened and who can tune
              into the higher levels of mind; and

shambhava: to one whose total identification is spirit-
(spiritual)   ual and divine and whose consciousness
              is so opened inwardly that it offers no
              resistance to the guru's force of Grace.

A subsequent text defines these as follows:

The *anava* method is that in which the initiate experiences an infusion through the external, physical means such as recitation, ritual movement, concentration, imagining the locus of the syllable, etc.

The *shakta* method is that in which the initiate experiences an infusion simply remembering the mantra with the mind without any recitation.

> The *shambhava* method is that in which the initiate experiences an infusion, without any effort at a thought of one's own, but simply awakened by the guru (internally).
>
> *Malini-vijaya Tantra II.21-2*

The readers will recognize the level they are at by comparing the above descriptions with their own experiences. One may also oscillate between different levels from time to time depending on the force of one's *samskaras.* According to the same text (II.24) there may be one hundred and fifty in-between states.

Looked at carefully, the texts above are describing both the level of initiation as well as the experience of the depth of meditation when one is tuned in to one's mantra. The initiating guru observes the level of consciousness and the capacity, *adhikara,* of the disciple and then initiates him into the level specifically appropriate. It depends on the personality's self-identification. According to the Shiva-sutras of Vasugupta a person at the *shambhava* level knows that "the body, *prana,* mental intelligence or even the annulment of these is not the self" (Kallata's commentary) but that

> *chaitanyam atma*
> Consciousness is self. I.1

To such a person

> the experience of the power of mantra
> occurs through diving into the great reservoir. I.22.

That experience is no other but total universal I-ness, an identity with the purest Supreme Consciousness which is *the* great reservoir. "This identity is (his) great mantra," says Kallata, and "is *the* power hidden in all the mantras."

A little less fortunate are those at the *shakta* level. To them

> *chittam mantrah*
> the mind is mantra. II.1.

Their mantra is not the identity with the Superconsciousness but with the mind alone. At the highest level of their experience, the entire mind becomes permeated by and identified with the mantra vibration. This is achieved through what is

> *prayatnah sadhakah*
> an effortless endeavor as the means
> of achievement. II.2.

The mind takes to the mantra naturally, and often the mantra permeates all the conscious and unconscious levels of the mind. For them

> *vidya-sharira-satta mantra-rahasyam.*
> the secret of the mantras is the identity of the
> syllabic measure with the universal energy. II.3.

The mantras bring them into contact with the universal consciousness which slowly begins to flow into the mind. For those at the *anava* level

> *atma chittam*
> the limited mind is the self. III.1.

They see "that personality as the self which is involved in all the worldly efforts of intelligence, ego and the mind." Their self becomes, according to Kallata, "atomic, little, transmigrating in incarnations through many species." Their

jnanam bandhah
limited knowledge of self is the bondage. III.2.

These three levels of the infusion of conscious energy experienced as

initiation, or
deep meditation

may be compared to the *pashyanti, madhyama* and *vaikhari* levels of speech which have been discussed earlier. Most initiates in the Himalayan Institute are familiar with an initiation process of a few minutes when they receive the mantra. In the ancient tradition, however, a would-be initiate went through a lengthy process of mental preparation, including fasting, meditation, ascetic observances, and celibacy, for many days, weeks, months or even years. Once admitted into the tradition, he belonged there. We read in the *Tibetan Book of the Dead* that the guru's reach is all the way into the next life; that the initiate who has practiced his mantra deeply will keep it even all the way through the *bardos,* the states between death and re-birth; that the guru may direct the process of entering the next womb if the initiate's *karma* leads him to reincarnation. The guru leads the initiate into enlightenment and liberation when the process of purification is actually complete. At the present time, the initiators have the duty to advise the applicant to postpone his mantra initiation until, in the initiator's opinion, his mind is ready at least to make a resolve to concentrate the mind in meditation, to sit for meditation daily, preferably at a fixed time, and to completely forswear the use of substances like marijuana.

The long preparations and purifications as prescribed in

the ancient traditions are not required at present because the
seed needs to be scattered widely, even if some fall by the
wayside. In ancient times the student requested admission to
the guru's lineage or the ashram, by approaching the guru and
offering him three pieces of kindling. The guru asks:

> Whose celibate initiate *(brahmacharin)* are you?

The disciple replies:

> Your honor's.

The guru says:

> You are the initiate of Fire *(agni)*.
> You are the initiate of the Masterful self *(Indra)*.

In other words the guru is not merely a person; he reminds the
initiate that the power known as the guru is the very fire of
consciousness within himself. To align himself with this internal
fire, the Masterful self, the universal guru, not only should the
initiate purify all his elements and senses but also totally open
himself to the guru's help during the entire purification process.

An initiation is not only a ceremony of simply receiving
the mantra, but includes *bhuta-shuddhi,* purification of elements. Here we paraphrase in brief the formulae for *bhuta-
shuddhi* from the most authentic text in this area, *Sharada-
tilakam* and its commentaries. (III.18ff.).

> The initiate has prepared himself and is sitting in the
> lotus posture, in silence, concentrating, having
> conquered his senses.

> The guru guides his consciousness through
> the steps indicated below.

> Applying the method of yoga as taught by
> the guru, with reverberating the sound of *hum,* on
> the *sushumna* path of the *kundalini* he unites his
> life-self *(jivatman)* to the Supreme Self *(paramat-*

man) with the mantra of consciousness *(chit-mantra: soham).*

The wise man should contemplate the lifeself through a dot in the artery of knowledge that arises from the Brahman-bulb in the heart lotus. It rises to the abode of the Supreme Self in the thousand-petal lotus.

Then he contemplates all the elements,

earth,
water,
fire,
air,
space, and
mind,

which are manifest in the six lower centers during creation, as remaining dissolved in the Supreme Self in the seventh center.

Now the process of creation begins. The initiate assigns the letters of the seed-mantras of each element to their respective centers.

With the seed-mantra of *prana* he inhales.

Imagining the personification of all his inner evil in his right side belly,

with the retention of breath,
with the fire-mantra
he contemplates as though burning to ashes
his evil person within.

Again with the seed-mantra of air he exhales the ashes of the evil person from within himself, scattering them abroad.

One thus purifies his person through this process of drying up, burning, flooding out the evil person. He establishes all fifty syllables, variants of one sound, into his entire person. He unifies them in the reverberation of *Om* which is *amrta,* the shower of the nectar of immortality. In the rain of its sound, with the water-seed mantra, he bathes his entire person.

In the process of creation—the division of higher consciousness being brought into the aspects of the person—he establishes the syllables from *a* to *ksha* into their assigned centers.

With the *soham*-mantra he draws down into the heart-lotus the individual life-self from the Supreme Self who dwells in the thousand-petal lotus.

Having thus seen that all the elements reigning in the centers of consciousness and in the physical person are descended from the Supreme Self in the thousand-petal lotus, he now makes the resolve for *bhuta-shuddhi,* the purification of elements. He contemplates:

> So, that I may be worthy of worshipping the Lord, I resolve upon purifying all my elements.

He observes the *kundalini* as arising from the first center, *muladhara.* She is brilliant like a thousand lightnings, slim as a fiber from the lotus stalk.

By following the path of *Sushumna,* he raises the *kundalini* into the heart center. From the heart lotus he takes the individual life-self *(jiva),* which is like an ember from the end of a burning wick. He raises it from the twelve-petal lotus of the heart into the thousand-petal lotus. With the *soham*-mantra he thus unites the *jiva* to the Supreme Self.

From the thousand-petal lotus he lets his Will descend. Having recognized this descent as the origin of his creation, *he now begins the upward ascent of energy and takes to the path of dissolution,* contemplating as follows.

From the toes to the knees*
a square, yellow of color,
is the mandala of the earth element.

In this realm I bring under control the

feet,
the act of movement,
goals to be arrived at,
odors,
the sense of smell,
the earth,
Brahma, the progenitor,
nivrtti-kala, aspect of withdrawal,
the *samana prana,*

Applying the mantra efficacious for the conquest of
the above realm.
　　By the path of the *kundalini* I raise all these
from the realm of the earth element and dissolve
them into the realm of waters.

From the knees to the navel,
crescent-shaped, white of color,
is the mandala of the water element.

In this realm I bring under control the

hands,
the act of receiving,
flavors,
the sense of taste,
waters,
Vishnu, the Preserver,
pratishtha-kala, the aspect of establishment,
the *udana prana;*

---

* The scheme of the seven *chakras* in this series of initiations is for a total beginner. Let
the reader not feel that it contradicts the more popularly known but actually the more
advanced scheme.

applying the mantra efficacious for the conquest of
the above realm.

By the path of the *kundalini* I raise all these
from the realm of the water element and dissolve
them into the realm of fires.

> From the navel to the heart,
> triangular, red of color,
> is the mandala of the fire element.

In this realm I bring under control the

> organ of elimination,
> process of elimination,
> objects to be eliminated,
> the sights,
> the sense of sight,
> lights,
> *Rudra (shiva)* the Dissolver,
> *vidya-kala,* the knowledge aspect,
> the *vyana prana,*

applying the mantra efficacious for the conquest of
the above realm.

By the path of the *kundalini* I raise all these
from the realm of the fire-element and dissolve
them into the realm of airs.

> From the heart to the eyebrows,
> circular, blue of color,
> marked with six points,
> is the mandala of the air element.

In this realm I bring under control the

> organ of pleasure,
> experience of pleasure,
> objects of pleasure,
> the tactile sensation,
> the sense of touch,

airs,
Ishana, the Ruling One,
shanti-kala, the aspect of Pacification,
the *apana prana,*

applying the mantra efficacious for the conquest of
the above realm.

By the path of the *kundalini* I raise all these
from the realm of the air element and dissolve them
into the realm of space.

From the eyebrow center to fontanella,
circular, clear of complexion,
is the mandala of the space element.

In this realm I bring under control the

speech (word, mantra),
process of conveying,
subjects spoken of,
sound,
the sense of hearing,
Sadashiva, the Transcendent God,
shanti-atita kala, the aspect beyond Peace,
the *prana,*

applying the mantra efficacious for the conquest of
the above realm.

By the path of the *kundalini* I raise all these
from the realm of the space element and dissolve
them into the realm of *ahamkara,* the ego.

I dissolve the ego into *mahat,* the great
universal Intelligence, the *buddhi* faculty.

I dissolve the Intelligence into *prakrti,* primordial Nature (the origin of nature's phenomena)
which is named *matrkas,* the syllabic measures, the
little mothers, that is *shabda-brahman,* the word
that is God.

After thus dissolving each lower mandala
into the successively higher mandalas, having

reached the highest, he *again begins the process of creation,* the downward descent of energy. He contemplates, and directs with efficacious mantras as prescribed in the Tantra, the

> descent of the powers of syllabic measures from the Word-God,
> descent of the powers of Intelligence from the Syllabic measures,
> descent of the powers of ego from Intelligence,
> descent of the powers of space element from the ego,
> descent of the powers of air element from the space element,
> descent of the powers of fire element from the air element,
> descent of the powers of water element from the fire element,
> descent of the powers of earth element from the water element,

each with their attendant associates, down through the highest to the lowest center of consciousness, from fontanella to the toes.

Once again, with process prescribed in the beginning, he again

> inhales,
> burns the evil personification from within his right side,
> exhales the ashes,
> floods them out, scattering them;
> takes a shower of the nectar of immortality.
> Thereafter he walks in the full knowledge that all the elements and aspects of his personal being, its acts and experiences are descents of grace from the Supreme Self. He knows "I am that"—*Soham.*

The reader is asked not to interpret the above process as
>ritual,
>
>poetry, or
>
>visualizations.

What has been summarized above, concealing detail that is beyond the grasp of the inexperienced, are initiatory processes at one possible level, out of many thousands of *kundalini* experiences imparted by the guru. He does so by touching the iron of the disciple's consciousness with the philosopher's stone of his own light. Like a lightning bolt it descends and transforms the disciple's base metal into gold. Of this experience the ancient Vedic seers proclaimed:

>*suvarna-jyotih:* I am the golden light.

The above *bhuta-shuddhi,* the purification of elements, may take years—the guru's grace touching one a little at a time. In rare cases it may come as it did to Arjuna in the middle of a battle-field as described in the chapters IX-XI of the *Bhagavad Gita.*

One receiving the mantra should read of the above process and learn of his goals. However, let him not become disheartened, saying:

>What is the point? I will never get there.

The greater guides will reply:

>Even though you may never climb Mount Everest, continue your lessons in mountaineering. Whatever you do climb will be an achievement. It is sufficient that before you die you become a person just a little more advanced than when you were born.

Sometimes questions are raised with regard to the presence of an incense stick or a candle flame at the time of meditation or mantra initiation. Let us refer here to a footnote by Heinrich Zimmer:

> The authors of *The Principles of Tantra* (edited by Arthur Avalon, 2 vols., London, 1914-1916), have aptly cited (pp. lxxi-lxxii) the following statement from the Council of Trent: "The Catholic Church, rich with the experience of the ages and clothed with their splendor, has introduced mystic benediction *(mantra)*, incense *(dhupa)*, water *(acamana, padya,* etc.), lights *(dipa)*, bells *(ghanta)*, flowers *(puspa)*, vestments, and all the magnificence of its ceremonies in order to excite the spirit of religion to the contemplation of the profound mysteries which they reveal. As are its faithful, the Church is composed of both body *(deha)* and soul *(atman)*. It therefore renders to the Lord *(isvara)* a double worship, exterior *(vahya-puja)* and interior *(manasa-puja)*, the latter being the prayer *(vandana)* of the faithful, the breviary of its priest, and the voice of Him ever interceding in our favor, and the former outward motions of the liturgy."
> (Interpolations by authors of *The Principles of Tantra.)* As to the historical relationship of the Christian to the Tantric service, that is a delicate matter yet to be investigated.
> *Philosophies of India, 586* [n.]

In other words, there is nothing eastern or western about these symbols. They help to create a sublime environment only for those who respond to them. If a candle, incense, figure of Jesus on the cross or the meditating Buddha and such other symbols invoke a response in an initiate's mind they may be used, but if one's associations, acculturations or beliefs resist their presence, they should be avoided.

12

The Character of an Initiate

One often hears a question asked, am I ready for my mantra? Or a statement, I don't think I am ready yet. The question is also raised as to what preparations are necessary for a would-be initiate before he requests a mantra. We shall try to answer these questions in the next few paragraphs.

The mantram is given to a student with a view to helping him in the following ways:

1. reducing the effect of and replacing a negative trait in the psychological personality, and
2. awakening the positive traits.

It is not that the different syllables or parts of the mantram have effects on different traits, but it is the combined sound vibration that brings the requisite modification in the mind. Like prayer, your mantra may be practiced:

sakama—with a desired goal in mind, or
nishkama—without a desired goal, with a sense of surrender to the Divine will.

In the Himalayan Yoga tradition one does not normally practice a mantra with the *sakama* view, desiring a fruit and hope that through this given practice one shall obtain a loving wife, receive the gift of a child, become rich, build a house, defeat an enemy, win a court case, and so forth. The guru may at times assign special observances to the student that will have such beneficial worldly effects. Such an observance may expedite the ripening of the disciple's *karma* or somewhat expiate it. However, in the student's mind there should not arise the issue of fruition and success with regard to material desire. The Himalayan Yoga tradition is dedicated to the liberation of human spirit from all want and dependencies. One's undertakings are without expectations. Therefore, when one sits down to practice meditation let him resolve only to be liberated from the ignorance which is the cause of all pain. Even in that resolve there remains constantly the confirmation of the prayer:

Thy will be done, and not mine.

When one practices the mantra in this way the results are fourfold:

1. *shuddhi:* purification of mind and personality so that the undesirable emotions and psychological traits, uncontrollable urges and impulses, are expunged and the person is purified;
2. *buddhi:* awakening of intelligence and intuitive faculty;
3. *siddhi:* attainments; and
4. *mukti:* liberation.

All these four are interrelated. Without purification of mind it is not possible for one to awaken the appropriate use of one's intelligence. Many times people complain of difficulties in business or inability to solve daily problems of life, though they are otherwise extremely intelligent persons. The reason for the failure is that the mind is disorganized. Through meditation the mind is cleansed of many blocks which have been preventing the flashing light of answers. As soon as one has freed oneself of angers, frustrations, habitual worrying and other such traits, the intuitive answers begin to arise and one is able to organize the mind's energy to foresee the direction of events and life developments many months and years ahead. Then one is able to plan appropriate action.

Siddhis, attainment of powers of all kinds, is a great temptation in the life of an initiate. The danger in the pursuit of *siddhis* is twofold:

1. At the slightest appearance of some hunch or some prediction coming through, and so forth, one begins to imagine himself as a *siddha,* an adept.

2. One becomes tied down to the desires for such powers and dreams of subtle ego. One might say, "Oh, if only I had the power to read others' minds I could help many more students." But deep inside the sub-conscious, there lurks the impurity which would not help the students but simply invade the privacy of their minds and derive from these invasions certain vicarious pleasures. Or one thinks, "If only I could predict which horse would win the lottery I could help my guru financially." One day I asked Swamiji,

"Why do you have to ask for funds? Why do you not simply buy a lottery ticket on a horse you know would win?" He told me quite sternly, "Don't you even think of that. Work honestly with your body. Work honestly to pay your *karma* and do not look for such easy ways out."

If one finds that special experiences or powers are coming one's way, the injunction is to conceal them carefully and not make your meditation group into a gossip club, every one vying with each other, everyone saying, "wait till you hear my experience!" The *siddhis* are not in fact any kind of attainments in the sense that they are additions to one's personality. According to the Yoga Sutras of Patanjali, they are simply the unblocking of power. As one advances on the path of meditation one begins to sense the presence of these faculties within. There is a great temptation to sit by the wayside watching this beautiful scenery of *siddhis* and if one does not resist, the path and the goal are forgotten. The recent trend in certain meditation circles to popularize *siddhis* and to sell them for a certain fee, is highly frowned upon by the masters of the Himalayas.

As you travel upon the path of meditation, you will sense the presence within you of power to help others. There are only three tests of whether you are making any progress at all:

1. During the meditation there is an experience of tranquility. No matter how shallow a meditation you have, how interspersed with the extraneous thoughts, you will arise from your meditation even slightly calmer than when you sat down.
2. In your relationships there will be unselfishness on your part, gradually less and less frustration, and greater peace of mind and joyfulness given by you to those around you.
3. Your presence will be helpful to others.

You should cultivate not powers, but the ability to help others in one way or another. For example, if a person comes in your presence with a disturbed frame of mind and leaves with a slightly calmer mood, it means you are succeeding in your meditation. Your voice will become more mellow, your posture expressing neither inferiority before those who are stronger than you nor superiority over those who are weaker than you. You are not trying to prove anything to anyone nor trying to impress someone. Simply maintain the four attitudes of frolicking in God.

As the practice of your mantra deepens your breath becomes calmer, and as the breath becomes calmer and deeper the entire *prana* force begins to vibrate within you. This vibrancy of your personality is not to be equated with the nervousness associated with displays of false energy. The energy is rather a calm presence that helps you to accomplish tasks for which previously you did not imagine you had the capacity. Your memory improves, your smile is infectious, you no longer desire to abandon situations of conflict. You become involved in the conflicts of others and succeed in bringing harmony where there was discord. You speak with great care only those words which are beneficial and pleasant and gradually whatever you say begins to come true. There is an affirmative power in your voice, *ojas,* so that others wish to listen to you and respond to you in a positive, loving or even adulatory manner. Well, here again you are in the traps of ego because you begin to bask in the sunshine of fame, honor and respect. Then you have blown it. Continue with your mantra, you have yet a long way to go.

The mantra is more or less the beginning of meditation. It may be safely said that in the Himalayan tradition there is no meditation without mantra. A complete beginner, of course, starts with using a word like *soham.* With the mantra initiation he enters not only into meditation, but into a relationship with the line of gurus through whose lineage the science of elevating the lower mind to the higher mind has developed. Mantra initiation, therefore, is given as early as possible. But of course it is necessary for the initiate to know:

What is a mantra?

What are its uses?

What changes will the meditation and mantra bring into one's life and relationships?

What is his relationship with the lineage of the gurus?

One of the derivations of the word mantra is from compounding the verbs *man,* to meditate or to contemplate, and *tra,* to protect, to guard, to be a guardian; i.e., mantra is that which protects one who contemplates it and meditates by it. It serves as his guardian and protector. If mantra is kept in the mind it serves as protection from the six internal mental enemies:

1. *kama:*   passions,
2. *krodha:*   anger,
3. *lobha:*   greed,
4. *moha:*   delusion, attachment,
5. *Irshya:*   jealousy,
6. *mada:*   pride, frenzy, or
   matsarya: small-mindedness, malice.

By maintaining constant remembrance, mental recitation, and concentration on one's mantra, one wards off the attack these six enemies make on the mind. The mantra serves as an antidote to these poisons.

In the long run for an advanced student, the power inherent in the mantra also invokes the presence of the universal Guru force, which protects the student from all manner of danger. Just as the unconscious destructive forces within us draw us to dangerous situations, so a positive force, well concentrated in our conscious being, draws us away from similar situations and produces a protective net around us.

The only preparation necessary before asking for a

mantra is as follows:

1. One should study a little of the background of the mantra initiation as we have explained in this book.
2. One should set aside a fixed time for daily meditation and resolve to be sincere in his observance.
3. He should sincerely wish to improve his life and relationships.
4. He should know that a mantra is kept completely secret and is shared with no one else.
5. He should understand his relationship with the guru lineage.

The mantra is kept a complete secret not because it is part of some kind of a secret societal rite, but for a purely spiritual reason. Human beings waste a great deal of energy in meaningless speech. The energy of mind is lost through unnecessary or loud utterance. This is no way of increasing the strength of the mind. It weakens and exhausts one, and leads to many unnecessary conflicts. We have spoken about the process of *sphota*, the movement of knowledge from the divine to the human sources, from the transcendental to the relative reality of articulate speech. The silence concerning the mantra is the beginning of a process of inward absorption of that energy, using the mantra as if it were a silver thread that leads to its own origins. Secrecy about mantra is a logical beginning of the practice of silence. We all know the power that a silently kept secret carries to create inward joy. One example is the secrecy surrounding gifts to be given at Christmas. What a thrill of positivity continues to run in one's mind until the gifts have been given! Mantra is a gift that the conscious mind passes on to the increasingly subtler layers of mind until it links us to our own source, awakening our reservoir of energy for integration into daily life.

Most people lead a life style in which their contact with space, time and causation is in discord. As a result, the music of cosmic energy with which the rhythms of personal human energy should be in harmony are ignored and we lead a life of dissonance. Our breath is meant to flow in definite rhythms so that all the other internal systems can function harmoniously. When a certain time and place is set for meditation, it is like a return to the beginning of the cycle of rhythms. When one has practiced meditation regularly at a certain time and place, the rest of life's pieces begin to fall into a logical order of sequence. Setting a fixed time for meditation and sitting at least once a day at that time will be extremely beneficial to the practitioner of meditation. As time goes on, its very subtle effects and benevolent consequences will be observed.

Of course there are times when it is not possible for a person to sit at a fixed time. For example, in the case of a mother with very young children or a traveler who cannot be at his meditation seat regularly. The advice given in such cases is that one should still resolve upon a fixed time. At that moment, even for one minute, while holding a crying baby or waiting in line at an airport, one still glances inwards at the fixed time and goes still and calm, paying a silent homage to the guru lineage and asking for the presence of their grace in one's life. Later in the day when the moment of immediate worldly necessity has passed and the circumstances are suitable, one may do one's daily meditation wherever and whenever convenient.

It is inconceivable at our ordinary stage of development to realize the grasp of forces the gurus of the Himalayan tradition maintain throughout their consciousness. Many years ago, H.H. Swami Rama called me over the phone from another city reprimanding, "Why are you reading the newspaper at your meditation time?!" Many others have narrated similar experiences—Swamiji calling and asking, "Why did you sit half an hour early? Do I have no other person to look after?" I once asked him how many people he checked on every night. He responded, "Between four-hundred to seven-hundred." I was astonished but he continued, saying, "Mind has no distance. It does not take time. It does not take more than a moment to establish contact with another mind." When such grace abounds on the part of the guru lineage, the least we can do is try to ignore our excuses or solve some of our problems so that we can respond to the presence of grace with a mind that is clear, clean, and pure. Through meditation, the mind can become a fit vessel to receive whatever drop of light is to be poured into us at that particular moment. Swamiji has often said, "I will help anyone who will sit at fixed times regularly in meditation." If you are prepared to give a moment of attention to your inward self at the time set for meditation, you can consider yourself ready to ask for a mantra.

The most important qualification that the gurus look for in a disciple is that he should be rich. He should be rich in what are known in the Vedanta tradition as six treasures. These six treasures are listed below.

Shama:	a quiescence, peacefulness of personality, a normally gentle temperament.
Dama:	self-control over one's senses of cognition so that the eyes and ears do not keep darting about helter-skelter without control and direction, and the hands and feet do not retain a nervous discharge of energy. One should be in control of one's thoughts, desires and emotions.
Uparati:	a feeling of withdrawal from the objects of desire and possessions of the world. This does not mean giving up all your involvement but simply realizing that

there are immediate duties to be performed *perfectly* and *lovingly*, without seeking the fruits thereof. One constantly prays and aspires for the time when one can renounce, even if it is into the seventh incarnation from now.

Titiksha: fortitude, forbearance. One should not constantly complain—it is too hot; it is too cold; someone has insulted me; I cannot stand this; I cannot bear that. The word *titiksha* simply means the ability to bear and absorb an insult and to accept discomfort *without feeling* that one is repressing one's natural urges.

Shraddha: a humble faith that one is indeed on the right path and that he has found a guide and a guru who will lead him to the core aspired for.

Samadhana: harmony and freedom from conflict. One should bring to resolution all one's conflicts within one's self through the practice of introspection, self-examination and the pursuit of right attitudes. Then one should bring resolution and harmony wherever conflicts appear in one's external surroundings and relationships.

This does not mean that you cannot ask for a mantra until you have reached perfection in all of the above six virtues! If you have already reached the perfection of liberation and enlightenment, why would you need a guide at all? What we are speaking of here are ideals one aspires for—the basic mode and pattern one wants to develop in his personality. The attitudes one should maintain in one's relationships, both worldly and towards the yoga tradition, can be summarized in three words:

service,
practice,
discipline.

One should be prepared to offer whatever service is needed by one's fellow human beings, by the individuals and families of fellow initiates and whatever can be given within one's capacity to facilitate the teaching mission of the guru. This requires pulling oneself out of an attitude of uninvolvement. One who serves with love cannot say, "I cannot become involved. I dare not make a commitment. I fear the consequences." One gradually learns to reach out not merely as a servant of the Lord, but even greater than that, a

dasanudasah, a servant of the servants of the Lord.

There should not be even so much ego that says I wish to serve only if God or my teacher or my fellow human beings will bring me close and near to them. Rather serve waiting at the door, washing the feet of those who are entering, not even asking to be allowed to enter. Regarding regular practice, we have already spoken about disciplines of the purity of mind which are as follows:

The four right attitudes:

maitri:	friendship and love towards those who are happy,
karuna:	compassion towards those who are in

	suffering,
mudita:	happiness at seeing others virtuous and making spiritual progress,
upeksha:	indifference towards the evil in others so that one helps someone out of compassion and love rather than because of the hatred towards evil in someone else.

These four are called *brahma-vihara,* that is "frolicking in God."

The five *yamas* and the five *niyamas* have been explained in numerous works on yoga. Briefly, again,

> nonviolence,
> truth,
> nontheft,
> control over sexual passion,
> nonpossessiveness,
> purity of body and mind,
> contentment,
> ascetic attitude, reducing one's sensual dependency on objects of desire,
> study of inspiring texts and silent repetition of one's mantra, and
> faith in God.

Mindfulness

> of one's posture,
> of one's breath,
> of one's emotions and thoughts,
> of one's mantra

should come naturally to a meditator. It is even more

important than meditation itself.

One may undertake special observances and disciplines from time to time. For example,

> 1) practice of silence—this means speaking
>   *hitam:* only what is beneficial to someone,
>   *mitam:* measured in tone, and number of words,
>   and
>   *priyam:* pleasant.

To practice speech by these three principles is more difficult than maintaining total silence.

One may also undertake the practice of total silence a few hours, half a day, or one day every week, according to the time and facility.

2) Fasting, that is, eating three mouthfuls less than enough to fill the stomach, is more difficult than skipping one meal entirely.

3) Tithing: after you have given, forget that you have given and it will come back to you. If you do not forget, it will not come back to you.

Practice these disciplines not as disciplines or punishments, but as pleasures that bring satisfaction and fulfillment of the heart.

Another type of discipline one may practice is called *prayashchitta,* or expiations. The formula recited for expiations is as follows:

> Whatever I have done that I ought not to have done,
> Whatever I have not done that I ought to have done, ·
> May it all be fulfilled by divine grace.

One may undertake the observances of expiation from time to time. The principle behind expiation is for the addition of good *karma* and better *samskara,* and to reduce the effect of negative thoughts, words, and deeds in the sum total of our personality constituents.

1) The transgressions committed with the physical body such as hurting, stealing, extra-marital sexuality, etc., are expiated by:

> giving charity,
>
> providing some service with the physical body,
>
> withholding sexual desire and activity for a given period of time,
>
> limited fasting by the definition given above,
>
> asceticism—or reducing one's dependency on physical comforts,
>
> giving away the possessions unnecessary to comfort that are mere instruments of ego, laziness, and leisure.

2) The transgressions of speech such as lying, gossip, hurtful words, are expiated through:

> practice of pleasant and measured speech,
>
> silence,
>
> chanting or singing holy phrases, prayers and hymns.

3) The mental transgressions which we commit continuously are expiated through the

> a) practice of *japa,* the mental recitation of one's mantra throughout the day and at the meditation times, and
>
> b) through the reading of inspiring words, scriptures, and biographies of great saints.

In practicing any of these disciplines two points are important:

1) One must practice them regularly and as often as

possible, but also set aside special periods in life for specific observances. For example, going to an ashram for a three-day practice of silence, or giving physical service to a cause for a certain duration of time. In other words, one must undertake a resolved act:

> I hereby commit myself to such and such discipline for such and such given period of time. May it be fulfilled and graced with success.

Having made the resolve one should attempt not to break it until it has reached its completion.

2) One must not practice these disciplines so as to discomfort someone else or neglect another important duty. If your husband, wife, child, parent, neighbor, teacher, student, guru, need your service or love—it is a transgression to sit down at that time to practice silence. Break the silence maintaining a calm frame of mind. Give your love and service without complaint, without letting them feel as if they burdened you. If you hold a calm frame of mind during that loving unselfish act it will be easy to return to your original silence. This applies to all of your practices.

Of course, one practices the discipline to which one can easily respond. If faith in God is not awakened at one time, surely it will awaken at another date. Meanwhile one may keep an open mind, and above all, unselfish love, a sense of gratitude and a feeling of humility. You have arrived at a group meditation and see a mother with a baby in her arms, uncertain and concerned about whether she should enter the room to meditate. If you pass her by for your holy meditation, you are not a great meditator. If, however, you approach her even though she is a stranger, and offer to take care of the child so that she can join the group in meditation, then you are indeed a meditator. If you arrive in the room and wait for someone else to lay down the carpet or sweep the floor, you are not a meditator, but if you go and ask for the broom and clean the area for others then you are a meditator. One constantly strives to pay his debt of gratitude, the *karmic* debt, towards:

> the parents and ancestors,
> the seers, gurus and teachers of the past,
> God and the forces of nature.

One pays the debt towards parents and ancestors by maintaining an attitude of humility and modesty in their presence, in spite of any differences of opinion. One may express a difference of opinion, certainly, but still exhibit basic respect, humility and love. The primary concern in one's relationship to the parents is that of serving them, taking care of their needs, and bringing them what joy is possible without trying to impose one's own view on them. This simple principle gives light to all kinds of situations in one's relationship with parents. For example, sometimes I am told by young people, "I now come to the Meditation Center but my mother wants me to go to the church. How do I resolve this conflict?" And my answer is: Where is the conflict? Why does your coming to the meditation group prevent you from going to church? In what way would your going along with your mother harm you while it is giving her happiness? You can still maintain your meditative attitude while you go through all the prayers, and they will become more meaningful to you. One who has not given service, love and joy to one's own parents, will not derive the greatest possible joy from other relationships. Many people who abandon their parents, unconsciously continue to look for a mother and father figure in a spiritual teacher. This will bring no lasting satisfaction. Our first relationship in life is with our parents. We should seek not to fail in that relationship so that we may succeed in others.

The debt towards the ancient seers and one's own guru and guide is paid by extending the teaching mission, either by striving to become a teacher oneself or by helping out in whatever other physical ways possible. According to the ancient traditions

> *diksha* will not bear fruition without *dakshina,* that
> is, an initiation from the teacher without an offering
> from the student is without its requisite complement.

The debt to the teachers, in other words, is paid

> 1) through one's own sincerity in service, practice and
> discipline as described above,
> 2) by trying to become a teacher if the guru considers
> you so qualified,
> 3) by making regular offerings of one's physical
> service, or through physical labor to the guru's mission.

We have mentioned above that the initiator and guru seek nothing from the disciple, but what about the student who is selfish? I recall in one lecture quoting an ancient text of *Ayurveda* stating that:

> a physician or a healer who charges a fee from the
> patient should be expelled from the Guild of the
> healers.

There was enthusiastic applause from the audience! But then I referred to another section of the same text saying that:

> a patient who will not take care of the physician's
> own physical needs and seeks to be healed himself

selfishly will not find permanent health.

This time no applause erupted from the audience.
The initiator, the teacher, the guide, the guru asks for nothing and expects nothing. That is his duty to himself, his payment of *karmic* debt to the higher ones in his lineage. An initiate and a student make it possible for the teacher to continue his service to mankind by lending a helping hand in whatever way possible.

The debt to God cannot be paid except by offering one's meditation to the living beings and saying to the Lord, 'Thy will be done, and not mine.' The debt to the forces of nature is paid by not exploiting it—by not polluting and not taking more than is necessary to maintain one's livelihood. We read in the *Bhagavata Purana:*

> *Yavad bhriyeta jatharam*
> *tavat svattvam hi dehinam.*
> *Adhikam yo'bhimanyeta*
> *sa steno dandam arhati.*

> Just enough to fill the stomach—
> this is the extent of the right to wealth;
> Anyone who would claim more,
> he, a thief, deserves punishment.

In other words:

> Prosper, so you may give;
> create wealth, so you may share.

Until all the *karmic* debts are paid off your meditation will not be pure and many extraneous distractions will continue to arise. The day no such thoughts arise in your meditation you are liberated and enlightened, but this will not happen until all your *karmic* debts have been paid off. Often the force of *karma* and the *samskaras,* the power of ignorance, are so strong that an initiate is incapable of overcoming the internal impediments by himself. For this reason, every qualified teacher and initiator prays for his students. The guru, of course, does so incredibly more intensively. They often do special mantras, dedicating its mental force to that of the beloved initiate. Of course, much depends on the initiate's worthiness and qualifications. To deserve such attention, to receive the fruits of the guru's prayer, the disciple must demonstrate a certain perseverance and commitment to his own practice. He had better be at his meditation seat at the time the guru is sending his prayers, grace, and the energy of his concentration towards him.

Sometimes a disciple charged with a mission and extremely busy with its duties may worry about not being able to spend sufficient time at his own practice. The guru is often heard reassuring him, "Why do you worry when I am doing the mantra for you!" A special type of mala, set of beads, may be used by the guru for such practice. In such instances the aspiring disciple finally quits the very idea of doing his practice for his own spiritual benefit. Out of a deeply felt gratitude for the guru's grace, he then follows the guru's example and dedicates his own practice for the benefit of his students.

Because no disciple under training can ever have the concentrated prayers for others that the guru says for him, the disciples have to find some other ways to express their overwhelming gratitude towards the guru tradition. The yoga tradition, therefore, teaches every student to dedicate his meditation to the guru lineage. In the beginning of each meditation session the initiate makes the resolve to sit for a particular period, or to say the mantra a certain number of times,

guru-prity-artham:

for the guru's pleasure

because it pleases the guru to see that the disciple is progressing. For a yet deeper expression the disciples may chant the *gurustotra,* an adoration to the guru which is in fact a hymn to the Divine teaching spirit of the universe. The yoga tradition also celebrates special days of devotion to the gurus, especially

guru-purnima:	the full moon day of July, dedicated to the guru,
shravani purnima:	the full moon of August, dedicated to renewing one's vows,
rishi-panchami:	the 5th day after the full moon of August, dedicated to commemorating the rishis, those seers to whose consciousness the mantras were revealed.

The student should therefore try to maintain certain basic disciplines in life, especially in preparation for meditation. These disciplines consist of:

Regular yoga exercise,
Cleaning the body before meditation, (If one cannot take a full shower, washing the feet, face and hands will suffice.)
Wearing clean, comfortable, airy clothing for meditation, (Natural fibers are preferable.)
And having neat and orderly surroundings, *especially* in the room where one meditates.

13

Power and Practice of the Mantra

The mantra is a powerpack contained within itself, and, like an atom, is a whole vibrant universe. Until one has a sense refined enough to investigate and to attune oneself to this subtlety beyond the realm of senses and dualistic rational thought, until one can rise to the intuitive flashes beyond the divisions of subjects, verbs and predicates, one cannot understand what is meant by the word powerpack, a *shakti-kendra,* or a point of energy *shakti-bindu.* This is comparable to a physicist who must concentrate high-powered beams of energy on a single atom before all the sub-atomic particles begin to show their presence. If the concentration of this energy continues, the *punctal* energy, *bindu-shakti,* of the atom called *anu,* bursts *(bhid)* on to an entirely different plane or level of existence sufficient to demolish an entire city.

This is the perfect simile for the concentration and expansion of energy, *sankocha* and *vistara,* of the universal energy as also manifest in the mind in mantra during meditation. The yogis speak of the expansion of consciousness yet advise the practice of concentration in meditation. Some students ask, "How is it possible for us to con*centr*ate on a single point and yet expect an expansion. An expansion connotes an outward journey, a concentration, an inward one. Is meditation an outward flow to permeate the entire universe, or is it a withdrawing from the universe to a single point of the self?" The answer given in philosophical texts will not be conveyed as clearly as the simple diagram below:

The movement of energy in the above diagram is in both directions: from the single point to the circle in expansion and contracting from the circle into the concentration of the point. It is this vibrant and dynamic interaction between the centers and the rims that constitutes all movement. There is only one difference—that the center point is always motionless, sending forth conserved but radiant energy into the outer rim causing the rim to move.

According to the Tantric tradition the center is always absolutely still like the calm eye of the storm. One of the mistakes being made in the field of physics today deals with this very problem. The movements of the electrons, etc., around a nucleus is seen only in a circular pattern, but the movement of the random particles is not necessarily either linear or circular, but has to do with the relationship between the central point and the rim. Such subtle forces of energy both of the unconscious and conscious realms are understood by masters in the highly secret path of yoga known as the solar science. If they were to let out this knowledge to the world, to the hands of the irresponsible, to those whose sense of morality has not been tested on the crucible of temptation and its conquest by ascetic endeavor, the world would be destroyed even sooner than the perimeters of time visualized by the politicians and the military men in power.

But back to the mantra! No *vistara* or expansion can occur without a *sankocha*—contraction or concentration. All the power of circular motion in a wheel is concentrated in the center point and it is from the stillness of the center point that it radiates out to the rim of the wheel. This is how the universe is run. This is how the micro-universes called the atoms continue to vibrate. This is also how the energy of the central point of the mind is expanded to permeate the entire body from which again it may be withdrawn into the core of the mind. Only when all the energies are thus concentrated on the single point of consciousness does a *bhedana* occur. *Bhedana* is the expansion which takes place on an entirely different level or plane of existence. That which seems to be a solid particle becomes an explosion of energy. All of this energy is concentrated in the *akshara-bija,* the syllabic seed which becomes the point of concentration into as well as the expansion from.

We may explain the power of the syllabic seed and its concentrated meaning by another metaphor. Pile a hundred pennies together to create the sum of a dollar. Weigh a single dollar against a hundred pennies. They weigh more than the dollar itself yet the value of the two is equal. Perhaps fifty pennies weigh more than a single silver dollar and yet their value is less than that of the silver dollar. All the power of the hundred pennies is concentrated in a single dollar which has less volume yet equal value. Gather together a cartload of pennies equal to a million dollars and send this cartload under heavy guard to your creditor to pay him. Only a malicious debtor would do such an act to pay back his creditor's money. However, if you want to be friendly, all you need to do is write a million dollar check and your signature is sufficient. The power of all the hundred million pennies is centered in your single signature which only authenticates your creditworthiness. The value is not in the volume of the cartload but in the creditworthiness. Similarily, the power of the mantra is not in a lengthy sentence or a heavy volume discussing its inherent philosophy, but in the power that the concentration on the mantra carries in the unmanifest and produces in the manifest as it is gradually realized.

Let us allow ourselves indulgence into one more metaphor. Many years ago I read a book on the CIA operations in many different countries. One of the chapters dealt with an operation in Poland where there was an American trade office. One of the officers was very fond of photography and would often travel around and take pictures of a harbor from a particular vantage point. The real purpose was to monitor the movement of ships in and out of the harbor. He would then dictate a fake trade letter, placing fake trade orders from other countries. The pictures of the harbor were miniaturized into a tiny dot the size of a period at the end of this sentence. One of the periods in the fake trade letter would contain the miniature photographs of the harbor. When the letter arrived at its destination in another trade office in Paris, one of the operators would scratch at all the periods in the letter and get the one that contained the pictures. It would be magnified and tell the story of the movement of ships in that particular Polish harbor.

The *point* of the story is obvious. (Pun intended!) The syllabic seed called the mantra contains within it many different pictures of the different levels of meditative experience. Until one arrives at the experience there is no point in trying to describe it in detail. It is like writing a book with all the scientific investigations about the nature, causes, physical correlates, etc., of sleep. It will be voluminous yet of no benefit to an insomniac. We may qualify that statement by saying that perchance the insomniac might fall asleep from boredom by looking at this overwhelming dissertation! Yet the dissertation does not contain the experience of sleep. Reading it is not sleeping. Similarly, translating a mantra is not experiencing it.

Let us return to our metaphor on the period point in the CIA letter. There is one difference between that kind of a point and the *shakti-bindu*, the point of energy, that the mantra becomes when it is assimilated into the core of the mind. The period point into which many photographs have been condensed, though minute, is constituted of the principle by which many parts make a whole. This is dismissed by the meditators as merely a *rajasic* movement of intellect leading to an inner restlessness, and conflict between the centripetal and centrifugal forces among those various parts. Even though to an observer that point is minute, within the self-contained world of that point, all those different parts have their own magnitudes of egos, no smaller than those of dinosaurs and dragons, of politicians devoted to intrigue, or to husbands and wives intent upon scoring points! That is certainly not the way of going towards the principle in consciousness.

The *shakti-bindus,* the points of energy, on the other hand are *sattvic* at worst. They are not made up of many parts, but of the complete undivided, indivisible, *nishkala,* without parts—single whole points that magnify but do not divide. Their magnification becomes the universe, creating parts into manifestations but withdrawing to the partless state. This state is also called *anu-bindu* which may be roughly translated as points of the minutest particles. The minutest possible particle, *anu,* is defined in the *Vaisheshika* system of philosophy as a point of no return, a point which can never be further subdivided without exploding into energy at another plane.

For the practitioner of the mantra it is essential that he gradually comes to this point of awareness, merging all the subjects, predicates, states of being and their modes called actions, into one singularity beyond which only energy patterns remain. Now, when much meaning is condensed into a few words during the process of an intuitive revelation relating to a given science—like the point in the period—the whole is constituted of highly condensed parts that comprise a philosophical statement. These statements are called *sutras* like the 195 Sutras of Patanjali or the Four Thousand Sutras of grammar by Panini, a predecessor of Patanjali. When no parts are discernible, such a *bindu* of consciousness-force is a mantra.

The practice of mantra is called *japa.* The purpose of *japa* is to let the mantra become a vehicle of your consciousness so that it leads you to the source of revelation, that *sphota,* the oneness of speech and energies with your own transcendental source. The mantra should be recited, repeated, remembered until it becomes part of your subconscious mind. Sometimes people say, "I cannot remember my mantram often." But you can remember your name so solidly associated with your person that if someone utters it in a crowd of one hundred people, your ears perk up! This is because you are so in love with your ego and identify your ego with your name.

The mantra is the name of the divinity within you. It is the name of the energy of consciousness flowing within you. Just as an arbitrarily chosen and artificially introduced name becomes so much a part of your outside personality, the mantra becomes an integral part of the subconscious mind. So let the internal name of the divine principle within you rise up from your interior and overcome the negative forces of your unconscious mind. Let your mantra, through constant repetition and remembrance become a part of your inner Self, to such a degree that it remains with you even in your sleep and dreams. Do not wake without it, do not go to sleep without it, but allow it to pervade the deep levels of your mind even when you are participating in extraneous activities.

The practice of *japa* may begin at a very low level of awareness. One may undertake to write down one's mantra a hundred thousand or a million times, resolving first to complete such an observance within a given period of time. We repeat, always with the intent to complete the observance within a given period of time. One may write one's mantra with a finger on one's palm without any ink. One may write it on paper, on a wooden board, a metallic sheet, or any such object specified by the guru. One may write it in color, or with a material such as sandlewood paste, also specified by the teacher. This practice should be done lovingly, almost calligraphically, making it an act of affection, as if one were writing a lover's name over and over again.

Some mantras are chanted in groups to create an atmosphere of sharing love and devotion. But in the yoga tradition one's own mantra is not chanted aloud. It is slowly refined through the stages as described below. Throughout these stages one observes how the mantram thought arises in the mind and how it is sent forth into the speech organs. It is only with such relaxed observation that one takes the mantra through the following stages:

Vachika:	articulated; one may mutter the mantram with one's lips as if saying something to oneself, observing how the thought arises from the mind and how it is sent forth into the speech organs. Gradually, one comes to the next stage.
Upanshu:	silent repetition in the mouth with sealed lips; here only the tongue moves but the observation of the mantra from the arising of the thought to coming into the speech organ continues. Then,
Manasa:	mental recitation; here the body is totally relaxed, the speech organ is completely silent, and the mantram is remembered only in the mind.

It is best that one does not have to go through the first two stages to reach the mental one. It is best if one simply relaxes all effort, sits in the prescribed mode of meditation with the gentle breath flowing, invoke or invite the presence of mantram, and experience the quiet remembrance. Do it lovingly, meaningfully enjoying the tranquility as it seeps into the rest of the person. One will become aware of many disturbing extraneous thoughts, but we have discussed this problem already in our previous work, *Superconscious Meditation.*

Gradually the mind enters a secret chamber, a cathedral whose dome is your skull. The mind sits as a worshipper using the mantra as though calling, calling, calling upon the divine lover to come and "be present within me." At this point let the mind become absolutely pleasant *(prasanna).* Let the mind be a silver bowl filled with absolutely still water, under the light of the full moon. Let your mantra be a pearl of purest light under the water, turning over and over and over again.

Go to the very core of your mind where the mind is linked to the will of the spirit (not to be confused with Will-power), the spirit of volition which creates a universe, that volition which runs the body and the mental personality without words. Ask,

Who am I?

By whose volition is the mantra thought sent forth? Observe the volition of the spirit, which is the same as the grace of the Golden Womb, sending forth the mantram into the mind. Here the mantram is not to be experienced as a combination of so many syllables. The entire mantram appears as a single unit, one's *sphota,* a burst of a particle of light, a single vibration. This can be explained by the following analogy.

If someone asks you what your name is, observe how the mind responds to the question. Because the name is a word most familiar to you, it does not arise letter by letter. The entire word is a single experience. Only when it rises from the *indeterminate* depths of your mind to the more *determinate* faculties does it become a loud thought made of letters and syllables. Let your mantra be experienced at that moment as a single flicker from the volition of the spirit. The entire mantra will arise once every second, twice every second, flashing, flashing, flashing. At that point it cannot be said whether it is a flash of light, a sound, or another mode of the energy of consciousness. Let the mantra become a single point of awareness, all else forgotten. Let it take you to the internal chamber of silence and be still.

> Amidst all your cries and laughter
> Let your mind take a moment off
> And go still.
> Look at this moment,
> This moment alone,
> And go still.
>
> This does not mean to silence
> All your thoughts, emotions and words.
> Just trace them to the silence
> Which precedes all speech
> And go still.
>
> There is a minutely brief moment
> Of quiet from which a wave rises
> And into which it merges;
> As you observe a wave
> Observe also its quiet source
> And the silent end,
> And go still.
>
> Each breath that you take

Begins and ends with a moment's pause;
Fill that gap when you breathe,
Fill it with the silence of meditation,
And go still.

Before you burst with anger,
Before you let go of your passion,
Hold your mind.
Fix it on a quiet within you.
Then even in the midst of anger and passion
You'll find a stillness that will make
Your emotions into a well-wielded tool,
A tool to help you
Be still.

At this moment dive within you.
Dive to the depths
And go still.

As the stillness in meditation deepens by centering
around a point which is the mantra, a centering will occur in
regular daily life. One remains aware of this central stillness
even when walking and acting through the day. Anywhere you
are, let this internal meditation continue.
    Devi said:

Merely by holding onto the mantra
In that very moment
Let him become absorbed, one with the mantra.
Here the very self of life dwells in the center
    of the coil of the *Kundalini*
As though a bud of light.
                    Matrika-bheda Tantra, XIV.1

This is a point where the mantra is no longer an effort
but without endeavor. This practice is called *ajapa japa*. A true
yogi does not practice the recitation or repetition of the mantra, but

rather listens to the inspiration of *sphota,* the continuous bursts of light being sent forth from within. A beginner practices *japa.* An advanced meditator simply remains aware of the *japa* that is going on naturally. To reach this stage, the grace of the guru's liberating mind is indispensable.

The practice of refining the mantra to an extremely fine point of awareness is indispensable for the meditator. Most people think their thoughts and utter their words without ever realizing or observing the processes involved. For an experiment, utter the sound of the letter 'a' or alpha as in the first letter of 'uncle' or 'under'. Simply say the sound 'a'.

Now articulate the same sound again while observing how the thought of the sound arises and what time it takes to produce the sound.

With this observation continue the repetition of the sound.

Now do the same, only with the lips, feeling the sound coming from the mind only into the throat and the mouth.

Now forget the speech organ and simply observe the arising of the letter 'a' in the mind.

Do this repeatedly in an unbroken chain of thought bursts of the sound 'a'. You will observe that the time that elapses becomes shorter and shorter and the burst of the thought of 'a' becomes quicker and quicker. According to the Tantras, the time it takes to recite mentally the sound of a single syllable is called an *akshara-matra,* a single syllabic unit of time. It is said in the Tantras that if one were to regard the time it takes the average person to think the letter 'a' in the mind as a single syllabic unit of time, a yogi in meditation experiences its refinement in 1/512th part of that time unit. When the mantra begins to reach such a refinement it ceases to be words and syllables and becomes a *bindu,* the word from which the English word 'point' is derived.

Bursting through the *bindu* is the next practice to which

the guru then guides the disciple. The purpose of *japa* is to reach this point of energy and to see this face of the mother of the universe

> who is the subtle essence, the syllabic measure, *devi,*
> the goddess, the deity of the mantras, the knowl-
> edge as the essence of the words and the syllables,
> the one beyond consciousness hidden within the
> aspects of knowledge, the witness of *shunya*—the
> emptiness of relativities among all things that are
> empty.
>
> *Devi-atharva, XXIV.*

By this process one reaches the very divinity that is the Word. By refining the word-consciousness into the Word-Consciousness

> when one sees the flashing of the self
> then it is called the supreme aspect *(kala);*
> she has now become the mother,
> she is called the *para,* the Transcendental Speech.
>
> *Yogini-hrdaya, I.36.*

Those who are on the path of *Nada-Yoga,* the yoga of sound, become absorbed simply in listening to the presence of the mantram, but the way to listen is again shown by the guru. Many people expect that the highest guru shall spend many hours giving instructions on meditation. Such instruction is necessary when teachers of lesser degree are teaching. In the presence of the guru all this becomes unnecessary, for once you have given him your sincere promise of keeping a meditation time and persisting in your search, the rays of the guru's consciousness will always touch you and will lead you from one point to the next, gliding ever so gently. He does not give instruction *on* meditation, he gives instruction *in* meditation.

When you have reached a point in your meditation

where the mantra simply flashes from within and a stillness occurs, you are now touching that half-measure syllable, *ardha-matra,* which is the silence experienced beyond the '*m*'of *Om.* It is disappointing that the words written here do not convey what is meant and one must await that ever-joyful experience patiently.

To most practitioners of the mantra meditation, the concept of a *bindu,* the highly concentrated point of consciousness, is a remote concept. By comparison, it is like someone writing Beethoven's Ninth Symphony when he has just only learnt about the octave. According to the Tantras, however, there are sixteen progressively advanced stages in the refinement of the mantra. Of these, the *bindu,* the dot as seen in ॐ *Om,* is the fourth and represents ½ of a *matra* or *mora.* At this stage the mantra is so refined that its vibration takes half the time that the most refined mental thought of the mantra might take in the practitioner. Here the *vaikhari,* the articulate enunciation, completely ceases and speech at the purely mental level begins *(madhyama).* The yogi immediately undertakes the practices that constitute shooting the entire awareness like an arrow targeted onto this central point. These are the practices of *bindu-vedhana.* Thereafter begins the attempt to burst through and beyond the *bindu.* It is called fission of the point, *bindu-bhedana.*

Onward in the discovery of the *bindu* are thirteen more stages until *unmana,* total transcending of the mind, occurs. Through these stages the vibration becomes more and more refined, splitting the *mora* successively into $1/2$, $1/4$, $1/8$, $1/16$, $1/32$, $1/64$, $1/128$, $1/256$, and finally at *unmana* the vibration is $1/512$ of the *mora.* In other words, a master's mind goes through 512 vibrations in the time it takes an average beginner to think his mantra at its most refined thought level. A yogi can do 512 thought-recitations of your mantra in the time it takes you to recite it once at the deepest level of your mind. The energy of such a vibration is intense and capable of reaching anywhere instantly and permeating any mind in the universe. When you have reached this *unmana* stage, you are entitled to be called a guru; *not before this.* One day I said to my Master Swami Rama, "It takes me three hours to reach the *bindu.*" He replied, "It takes me three minutes to do the same, and my master takes only three seconds."

If you can imagine a single point, the point that has location but no magnitude, as though it were a minute apple pie divided into 512 parts, you will understand what has been said above. These parts, containing enormous powers that control the vast functions of the universe and the mind, are called *kalas,* the calculables; from these all the measurable quanta and the data of time, space and causation proceed. When the pieces of the minute pie are no longer seen separate, the *bindu* is transcended. *Nada,* the sound beyond the universe, which is one with *jyotih,* the light beyond the universe, becomes the dwelling place of the yogi's consciousness, beyond even the individuated *kundalini,* in the heart of the Sun that shines in the core of the thousand-petal lotus. How many hills and mountains are there to climb between our Poconos and their Himalayas!

We have not yet explained the practice of the mantra with breathing. It is said that the breath in meditation is of two kinds. Nonpregnant—without mantra, and pregnant—with mantra. One needs to learn to impregnate the breath with the mantra so that the awakening of *prana* and the filling of mind may occur in synchrony. The mantras are of varying lengths and cannot always be synchronized with the breath. One should not struggle with this practice and should let it flow naturally. One's daily practice of meditation *should* follow this order:

1. Yoga postures,

2. Relaxation,
3. Alternate nostril breathing,
4. Sitting up and establishing diaphragmatic breathing.
5. Allowing the mantra to arise in the mind and adjusting the breathing to whatever pace feels easy and natural, however many times in the breath. Practice the mantra in the breath in this way for some time.
6. Then the breath may be ignored and the mantra refined and observed in the mind.
7. Enjoy the stillness and intermittent flashing of the mantra, leading again and again to the stillness.
8. Return to the breath, then back to the senses, to close the meditation.

There are many different modes of breathing for meditation. Some possibilities include breathing:

As though the breath is flowing through the whole body,
From the navel center,
From the heart center,
Between the navel center and the center between the eyebrows,
Between the heart center and the center between the eyebrows,
As though one is inhaling from the base of the spine and exhaling from the top of the head,
As though the breath is flowing up and down through an imaginary hollow in the spine,
The touch of the breath felt in the nostrils,
As though the breath begins where the mantra thought arises in the mind and flows through the nostrils,
As though the breath begins where the mantram thought arises in the mind, flows through the center between the eyebrows, not in the nostrils, but through the nosebridge to the spot where the nosebridge joins the upper lip.

This last is considered a very advanced practice called the *Sushumna* breath as taught by Swami Rama of the Himalayas.

This information alone is insufficient. It would be difficult for a student to determine which of these modes of breathing is most appropriate for him. Furthermore, as his practice advances he may also synchronize the practice of his breath and the mantra with certain yantras, visualizations of light, in the various centers of consciousness. It is therefore essential that the student remain in touch with the guru and the teacher's lineage and seek consultation from time to time.

It is by combining the practice of breath and the mantra on the path of the *kundalini* as taught by one's teacher, that the energy in the various *chakras,* the centers of consciousness, begins to awaken. When *prana* and the *kundalini* are thus experienced as unimpeded forces permeating the entire person, the mantra appears to be their vibration. The *prana* vibration becomes one with the mantra vibration.

> There is no one reciting it
> no one causing its percussion.
> This deity dwelling in the beings' hearts
> is impelling itself up, reciting itself.
>   *Svacchanda Tantra.*

Elsewhere we are taught:

> The mantras would be mere forms of words
> dwelling in the animal nature of consciousness;
> only when energized on the path of *Sushumna*
> (the central channel of the *kundalini*)
> do they lead to the union with the Lord.
>   *Hamsa-parameshvaram.*

As one absorbs the power of the mantra one may hear the

anahata, the unstruck sound in the heart, or may be led to the *nada,* or *surat-shabda,* the word into which one becomes absorbed in the cave of the bees. The latter is a pathway of consciousness leading to the music of the angels and the silence of pure divinity.

14

Your Mala Beads

The mala is the string of beads used as a timing device for one's meditation so that one does not have to look at a clock. Instead one advances one bead with each recitation of the mantra until one round of the mala is completed. Then one may start over again.

The word *mala* is very ancient. Even its origin in Sanskrit language is obscure. The word is perhaps not so much Indo-European as it is Indo-Pacific in its origins. It is pronounced in two ways in India: *mala,* in the North, and *malai* or *malei* in South India. Drop 'ma' and it becomes the Hawaiian 'lei' or the Samoan 'ole'.

There is an extremely ornate mala which may be woven of thousands of flowers in a myriad of colors, with mandala-like combinations forming different colors at various intervals. There are also many malas within malas. Some malas reach all the way down to the feet. Nor are malas simply garlands, but can be necklaces of pearls, stones, seeds and so forth.

The flower garland used as an offering to some honored guest is a tradition from Polynesia, across the Pacific, through the countries of Southeast Asia, and down to South India. There the mala or garland is open-ended and when it is placed on someone's neck it is tied behind his neck. It is given as a love offering as well as a worship offering. One of the traditions of India and the Pacific cultures is that what you offer a human being as an act of love, you offer to God as an act of worship because you honor the divine in the human. You do not use anything for the human purposes unless you first make it an offering unto the divine.

The distinction between the mala offering for love and worship, and the mala used for one's own wearing or for *japa* and such sacramental practice, is not a very clear one. There is a point where the ideas merge. In North India for example, one sees people selling these garlands outside every temple. You buy the garlands and make an offering of them at the temple. Similarly, at every airport in India the departure lounge is filled with flowers. Friends and family garland the departing or arriving guests. For some reason you are not allowed to take those garlands into the airplane so they are dropped there and cover the floors with petals.

Moreover, there are flower garlands with historical and cultural association. The color type of flowers for special occasions has its own rules of propriety and appropriateness. For example, when a certain worship is performed you bring the purest yellow flowers. In other instances flowers should be of a certain mandala-like design when used for offering. These stipulations can be understood by today's science as we study certain designs that appear and reappear in nature, from the structure of shells to the formation of the galaxies.

Now we set aside these garlands and necklaces and come to our simple one-hundred-and-eight-bead mala. It could be one thousand and eight beads. It could also be one thousand and eight flowers. But a one-thousand-and-eight-bead mala cannot be easily worn or used for reciting your mantra! There is a specific reason why it cannot be used for the recitation of the mantra which will also be explained.

We call our mala a *japa-mala*. The word *japa* means repetition of a particular mantra. *Japam* or *japa* is the process of reciting, repeating, remembering the mantra. This is done on many levels. When it is done with speech and mind, it is practiced in several different ways. For example, you may chant the mantra which many people do in traditions where chanting is recommended. Chanting may be done reciting the mantra, singing it, or becoming absorbed in the mantra's sound and whole mental feeling. You may also mutter the mantra with the lips without chanting aloud, or you can close the lips and recite it with the lips sealed but with your tongue moving. You can then stop the tongue and permit the recitation to become mental. Here, the mind remembers the mantra and lets it go on as naturally as possible.

The final stage, the highest stage is *a-japa japa,* the unrepeated repetition which is the state of the highest absorption in mantra leading to the inner central point.

Finally, as we have explained, the mantra is practiced in many other different ways: in the *chakras,* with the breathing, with the heartbeat, with the pulsebeat, to name a few. It is said that the shortest human breath possible would make twenty-one thousand six hundred breaths in one tweny-four hour period. So if you become used to the *a-japa japa,* the unrepeated repetition, you recite your mantra twenty-one thousand six hundred times in a day and night.

For people who are very devoted, for whom *a-japa* or the use of meditation is not only a mechanical relaxation tool, the *japa* is an *anushthana,* a sacrament, that is undertaken to meditate with a resolve for higher purposes. It is said that of all the sacraments, the sacrament of the silent prayer *(japa),* is the highest, the most effective, the most beneficial, and the most godly. If you have inner ritual you need no other ritual; if you have inner prayer you need no other prayer. *Sarve te japa-yajnasya narhatah shodashim kalam.* All the other sacraments and external offerings that you perform would not constitute even one-sixteenth part of the sacrament of inward worship which is *japa.*

One problem with symbols is that they cannot be explained on only one level. If you attempt to explain them on all levels there is yet another problem—people hear the explanation only at the level at which they themselves are consciously functioning. So the symbols remain associated in a person's mind with only one level and are rejected at other levels as though those other levels were meaningless. We will explore the mala at our present level of comprehension keeping in mind the great potential depth. You should accept what is right for your understanding in the present.

Where does it all fit into one? This is the importance of symbols: that one thing is many things. All interpretations of a symbol are true and they all are accurate.

The word *bead* is probably derived from *bija,* a seed. When you hold a bead in your hand you hold the *bija,* the seed, meaning that you hold all the branches, all the leaves that have ever sprouted or will ever sprout from its cellular structure.

A mala actually has one hundred and eight plus one, making one hundred and nine beads, joined together with a thread. The word 'thread' in the Sanskrit language is *sutra,* as in the Yoga Sutras. The English word suture is derived from the Sanskrit word *sutra:* a thread. This is that *sutra* that sutures those who are separated, joining them together.

> *Yo vidyat sutram vitatam yasminn otah praja imah*
> *sutram sutrasya yo veda sa vidyad brahmanam mahat.*
> *Vedaham sutram vitatam yasminn otah praja imah*
> *sutram sutrasyaham vedatho yad brahmanam mahat.*

He who knows that *sutra,* that thread into which all

of these beings are woven, and he who knows the
thread of that thread, he knows the great Brahman.

The great yogi says:

> Now I have come to know that thread into which all these
> things are woven. And I know the thread of that very
> thread also. Now I know Brahman.

The thread that passes through all of us, is that *sutra*
thread of one life. All our skulls are beads in the necklace worn
by the Great Dissolver. All our bodies are as beads in that
thread through which that one thread of *prana* and *atman* is
passing. All the moons, the stars, the earth, the planets and the
galaxies are the beads, and the thread passing through all of
them is the thread of the Inner Space, Divine Life. It is the *sutra*
as hidden statement which joins the vast multiplicity of the
forms of the universe. The *sutra* by which these innumerable
things are "*sutra*-ed," is the thread through all the beads of your
mala.

We need to understand the *sutra* thread of unity behind
the diversity of all the millions and millions of planets that I, the
Divine Being incarnate, hold in my hands. When you have
expanded your consciousness, then you do not hold simply a
few beads and a piece of thread going through them. You hold
the beads of all the planets of the whole universe in your hands.
The *sutra,* the thread, reminds you.

The thread in the mala is tied in certain ways. There are
two kinds of ties in the world, two kinds of binding forces in the
universe, two things that tie you down or tie you together.
Tying can be something that binds and limits you. Tying can
also be that which joins you with that one from which you were
separated. One kind of tie is called the *nagapasha* and the other
kind of tie is called *brahmagranthi. Nagapasha* is the tie of a
snake which binds one down to the world and to the snake of

the universe. *Brahmagranthi* is the tie of Brahman which unites us with God.

When preparing the mala, two and one-half knots are referred to as *nagapasha,* which is considered to be just a little short of this side of the trinity. When they speak of *brahmagranthi,* the Brahman-knot, they speak of three and one-half knots, which is on the other side of trinity. When we are short of trinity, it is two and one-half knots. When we have crossed the trinity and gone to the final unity, it is three and one-half knots because the final half is the silent, unmanifest, transcendental, which lies beyond the articulated sound of *Om.* When you are doing your *japa* you are aware of being tied down, but when you really reach the top end of the mala, the *meru,* then it is three and one-half knots.

In some malas there are knots in between the beads. In others there are no knots in between the beads which means that there is not that much separation. However, with the malas that have knots in between the beads, the knot should be very close and tight. Then there are other malas in which a silver thread or wire is used. Each bead has a link joining the silver link of the next bead. These are joined by hand and are very difficult to make. They are created in India by authentic mala makers who employ special mental processes in their making.

There are beads of ordinary wood, of *tulsi* (holy basil) wood, or of the sandalwood, to name a few. Then there are malas of certain specially prescribed seeds. You may also have malas of crystal, special gems, coral and so forth. A mala should be selected with as much care as a stone for a ring. One does not just go and buy a mala, wear it and use it. Some malas are matched with your mantram.

The most expensive and difficult malas to obtain are *rudraksha* malas. Literally translated, *rudraksha* means "the eye of the three-eyed one." These used to be imported from Tibet where the *rudraksha* tree grows in abandon. Since the

Chinese took over Tibet the *rudraksha* malas are no longer available from that area as all trade has been closed off. The second best tree grows in Indonesia. The fruit-like seeds are taken from the trees and buried for two years in the ground. After they are dug out, the skin is easily removed without damaging the seed. Then the seeds are selected according to size, washed and threaded. An ideal mala is one in which all the seeds are completely equal and even. It is a very difficult task to match one hundred and eight seeds out of thousands and thousands of seeds and have them of equal size, form and weight. There are special Brahmin families who traditionally perform this service. From these families, only the unmarried virgin girls thread the malas. When the mala is really made conscientiously a certain *gayatri* mantra is repeated for each knot. When they reach the top bead there are further mental observances. Upon completion, the mala is taken through special sacraments in which they are dipped in holy water while incense is burned. They are then brought out and made available to the public. Some *rudraksha* seeds have five different faces which represent five aspects of special *shivaman-tras* which are normally practiced with the *rudraksha* beads. To go into the symbolism of each one of these would take many, many years, because you have to delve into the entire science of mantra. It would be like trying to match a stone to someone's personality and then exploring the astrology involved.

To shed light on the reason for the mala consisting of one hundred and eight beads, let us summarize what we have explained elsewhere in the book. The entire capacity for sound was divided by the ancient grammarians into fifty letters. Of these, sixteen are vowels, which are the feminine aspect of the language. Once again let us see the alphabet.

Vowels

A ā i ī u ū
r ṛ ḷ ḹ
e ai o au aṁ aḥ

Consonants

guttural
K group: K̲ kh g gh ṅ

palatal
Ch group: C̲h̲ chh j jh ñ

retroflex
Ṭ group: Ṭ ṭh ḍ ḍh ṇ

dental
T group: T̲ th d dh n

labial
P group: P̲ ph b bh m

semi-vowels: Y̲ r l v

sibilants: S̲h́ ṣh s

aspirant: h

special conjunct: kṣh.

As is clear, the alphabet is divided into various phonetic
groups, as follows:

(1) Group one, the vowels, starting with 'a';

(2) five gutturals (letters of the 'k' group, ka, kha, ga, gha, and the nasal sound *ṅ* as in king);

(3) five letters of the 'cha' group;

(4) five letters of the hard 'ṭ' group;

(5) five letters of the soft 't' group;

(6) five letters of the 'p' group;

(7) the semivowels 'ya, ra, la, va'; and

(8) the sibilants 'śh, ṣh, s', an aspirate 'h', and one letter representing joint consonants 'kṣh'.

This makes a total of fifty letters. In the one hundred and eight beads of the mala the first one hundred are fifty repeated twice and the last eight are the group leaders: A, K, CH, Ṭ, T, P, Y, ŚH, the first letter of each group, shown in underlined capitals in the chart above. In this way the entire alphabet is repeated three times in the mala.

These are all the possible sounds into which language can be divided. Those sounds themselves were divided in a certain physiological order. First, all the vowels in the order of short vowels, long vowels, diphthongs and so on. Next are guttural sounds, spoken from inside the throat, coming from inside and moving outwards; (The Indians always thought of going from inside outwards); the palatal sounds; the retroflex, hard t sounds; the dental sounds; and the labial sounds. The final consonant of each consonant group is a variant of the 'm' sound representing silence. ("Mum's the word," we say in English.) The entire language divided into fifty units repeated three times becomes one hundred and eight. This is one possible explanation of the one hundred and eight beads.

The entire alphabet of these fifty letters was further divided and subdivided and associated with one hundred and eight parts of the horizon. The ancient Indian astronomers divided the entire horizon into twenty-seven parts, the twenty-seven constellations, through which the moon travels in a month. Each of these twenty-seven star clusters is divided into four quarters. Twenty-seven times four is one hundred and eight. When a child is born we give a name according to the moment of his birth. Every child has an astrological name as well as special birth stones, horoscopes and charts.

Because language is organized according to a cosmic principle, the first letter of a newborn child's name is decided according to where a particular letter of the alphabet falls in association with the movement of the moon through the horizon, each letter, each sound, each syllable representing a cosmic force. Also when a person is initiated into yoga, the moment of his initiation is a new spiritual birth, and he may be given an initiate name according to the position of the moon at that time.

Before we get carried away by the astrology let us understand that there is in yoga a science which may be called micro-astrology. The moon, the sun, the twenty-seven parts of the horizon and the twelve signs of the zodiac are not anything external. They are all states of breath associated with the mental forces which a given syllable in language represents. That is a very, very fine science of which Swami Rama is a master. Just by watching the state of your breath he can calculate many things about your life. From the position of the moon in the particular sign in your breath he would say, "This is in the future," or "This is the question you want to ask me." Again, it is obvious that the universe is multi-dimensional. What sounds completely silly at one level—astrology and superstition, for example—sounds feasible at another level.

There is a third possible explanation for one hundred and eight beads. Since our mantras are so closely united with breath, let us look at the number of breaths in *nadi-shodhana,* the exercise of channel purification.

Round 1   Round 2   Round 3

| Active Nostril | Passive Nostril | Active Nostril | Passive Nostril | Active Nostril | Passive Nostril |

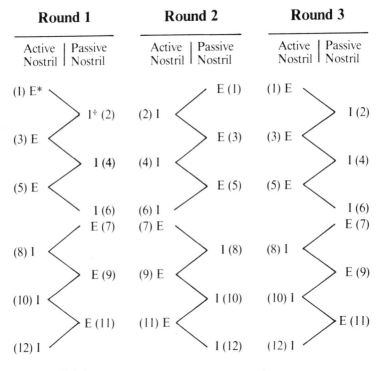

*Exhale   †Inhale

Three "rounds" as described above consist of thirty-six exhalations and inhalations. Each of these thirty-six breath cycles is repeated in the morning, at noon and in the evening. Thirty-six times three is one hundred and eight. If you do the entire process described above in one sitting, you also have one hundred and eight.

We have presented some descriptions of the significance behind the number one hundred and eight. I suspect there are other explanations also.

When we do our *japa*, as an *anushthana*, with a certain resolve to sit down and complete a specific number of repetitions, the mala is a better time keeper than a clock. One does not want to be thinking about the time when going to the timeless. With the mala it is much easier to sit down and say 'I'll do five hundred repetitions', and do five mala rounds. The last eight beads of the mala are not taken into account but they make up for the mind wandering off.

In Chapter Five we have explained the meaning of the word *aham* "I", and that it incorporates the spiritual and mental principles of the forty-nine syllables of the alphabet as they occur in the petals of the *chakras*. We have shown how the speech principle

begins with the letter *a* in the throat center,

the consciousness travels down through the *chakras* to the syllable *sa* in the lowest center,

then travels up with the breath to *ha* or *ham* in the sixth center between the eyebrows, and that

this entire journey constitutes the meaning of the thought *aham*, 'I'.

The mala held in the hand would represent this one cycle of breath but there is a further qualification. *Aham*, 'I', *a* to *ha* represents the inward journey of consciousness. A realistic philosophy must make accommodation for the outward journey of consciousenss, too. The yogis have placed a conjunct syllable *ksha* also in the sixth center. It is not a pure sound but a combination of *k* and *sh,* aided by the vowel *a.* This represents the conjunct and impure state of outward consciousness, the senses opening outwards. '*A* to *ha'* represents the inward journey but when the physical body experiences its relationship with the universe through the senses, the fiftieth letter *ksha* comes into play. Then we speak of consciousness and the speech principle moving from *a* to *ksha,* uniting spirit with matter. Thus the Sanskrit word *aksha* means the senses, and *akshi* means the eye which represents the cognitive senses in the philosophy.

This brings us to the word *rudraksha,* a compound formed from *rudra* and *aksha,* which the uninitiated may translate as the eye of Rudra or Shiva. In fact it means all that may be included from *a* to *ksha,* spirit to the physical senses acting within the Shiva Principle, the Deity meditating within us. It is thus that the Sanskrit word for the alphabet also is *varna-mala,* which means the mala, garland or necklace of *varnas* or syllables. The *japa-mala* represents the *varna-mala,* each syllable joined by the thread of breath passing through the centers of consciousness. It incorporates the life-energy flowing through all the *chakras* and the potentiality of all the mantras therein.

The top, one hundred and ninth bead is called *meru,* which is the central mountain of the universe, the spine itself. It is said that on the two sides of this mountain the sun and the moon, the solar and the lunar breath in yoga, rise and set. This bead is also called the guru-bead or God's bead.

There are certain simple rules about the use of the mala. There are many reasons for such traditions but many people do not know or observe them. The tradition is that the mala used in practice should not be worn but kept on your meditation seat or in your pocket. Normally, in a very strict ashram discipline the two would be kept separate. When in use, the mala should not touch the floor or make sounds. Some people have extra long malas and allow them to click-clack so that everybody knows a great devotee is doing *japa!* There should be no sound. You should not treat the mala casually. Use it with respect and discipline.

There are two different statements about the relationship of the mala to the *chakras.* One is that you may hold it so that the *meru* is the starting point in front of the eyebrow center. Another option is to hold it in front of the throat center. In this manner the mala does not hang down below the navel center, so one's consciousness symbolically remains above this point.

However, with the normal sized mala this is very difficult. It is also awkward to hold the mala at the eyebrow center and turn the beads in that position. If you locate it in front of the throat center, it is still inconvenient because the hand has to be raised and you cannot fully relax.

Another method is to hold the mala so that the *meru* bead is in front of the heart center where it represents devotion. This is the most common technique. For this practice, you form the *japa mudra* by holding the mala in the right hand and letting it fall into the open palm of the left hand which rests in the lap. Ideally it should rest above the navel but that would distract a beginner.

When you are no longer using the mala, place it across your right knee or on your meditation seat by your right knee. Do not dump it on the ground. For meditation every act should be for a meditative purpose—an act of restraint, watchfulness and discipline. If the mala breaks it should be restrung with a pure mind and perhaps blessed by the Guru, or initiator. Through this blessing his vibrations are relayed through the mala and on to the initiate.

When people sit for long meditations, they may be advised to keep a water vessel made of silver, copper or brass, close at hand because the throat gets dry. The water in the water vessel of a person who is deeply meditative has healing qualities. (The mala may be placed on the right side along with the water vessel.)

Holding the mala, let it hang on the little depression of the ring finger. The index finger is tucked away in a *mudra* inside the crease of the thumb and the mala is moved between the thumb and the middle finger. Traditionally, it is considered better to use only the thumb in moving the mala.

When you have reached the top *meru* bead, you do not cross it. *Meru,* the one hundred and ninth, represents transcendence. *Meru,* then, represents the middle path of the Center within, the *Sushumna* or the central channel of the *kundalini,* the Guru and God, and therefore must not be transgressed. For this reason, during *japa* when the fingers reach the one hundred and eighth bead, one turns the mala around and begins again. You are not yet at a point where you can go over the guru's head!

There is a correlation between alternating direction of the mala and alternating the direction of the breath—left to right breath then right to left breath symbolic of the flow in doing *nadi-shodana,* the channel purification.

There are other types of malas. The *sumarni* mala has only twenty-seven beads and does not have the top guru bead *(meru).* That mala is used for the practice of *ajapa japa,* or the unrepeated repetition that goes on without a break. When the *sumarni mala* is suggested for use, it is said that the hand should continue moving without a break all through the twenty-four hours. Even in deep sleep, it continues moving. Because this type of mala does not have the break of the *meru* bead, it is most suitable for doing *japa* in continuous cycles. One may make a special *anusthana* (resolve) of never breaking the *japa* no matter what you are doing.

One may also use the fingers of one's right hand as a mala. The counting is done as follows, using the tip of the thumb to touch the various points.

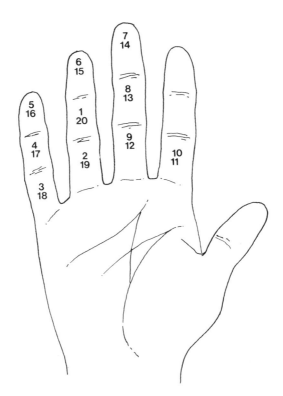

The tradition has it that during the day one uses the hand for this purpose keeping the palm up. At dawn and dusk the palm faces the heart, and after sunset the palm faces down.

The mala is kept concealed like the mantra. It is kept, held or used as unobtrusively as possible. This is a good basic principle to follow in life—be humble, keep all signs of goodness and holiness hidden.

Except when you are doing *japa* in a group the practice should be private. Like your meditation seat, like your mantram, it is personal. It is your secret. When you are with others and want to do your mala, you can wear a shawl and conceal it underneath. Be discreet. In India there is a special sack called *gomukhi.* You put your hand and the mala inside the L-shaped cloth while moving the mala.

In human beings there are certain natural rhythms. An experiment was conducted in the hospital room where newborn babies are kept. The control group had no sound. The other group had the sound of a heartbeat broadcast nonstop for four days, and in another group the heartbeat sound was at a faster rate. The group in which it was faster cried all the time, and the group that heard the normal heartrate cried significantly less than the control group. A child becomes used to the heartbeat inside the mother's womb. It is his most reassuring sensation. If you are trying to put a child to sleep, put him on your left shoulder so that he can feel the heartbeat. Children develop all sorts of ways of responding to certain natural rhythms. Adults have unfortunately given up any kind of association or assimilation of consciousness with our inner rhythms such as heartbeats, pulse rate and so on.

When beginners meditate they go from frequency to frequency, alpha to beta to theta, alpha to beta to theta to alpha to beta, and then off they go exploring the whole world. When this occurs the brain waves move in a jerky fashion. Since the mind tends to go out into your active senses, the movement of the hand in *japa* is an excellent release while keeping the rest of the body still.

Meditation has been described as the continuously unbroken flow of one single thought. Your mantra should move in a pattern; you establish a rhythm and then you refine it and let it move at the same rhythm, at the same rhythm, at the same rhythm. Let the movement of the mala in your hand release any hidden tension. Anything in the mind going out into your active senses is also released at the same rhythm so there is a symmetry between the rhythm of the active sense and the rhythm of the inward consciousness. After a while, the two become so closely associated that when you hold the mala in your hand you go inwards. Through that association you immediately establish that rhythm in the mind. As you refine your meditation, it takes less and less time to repeat the mantra and your point of concentration becomes finer, finer and yet finer. The movement of the mala should follow the mind, not the mind follow the mala. When the mantra becomes a fine vibration, the mala helps to make the repetition of that vibration even. When each bead represents one recitation, one heartbeat, one pulsebeat, one syllable, in meditation, your mind becomes like a crystal bead rolling over and over and over and over as though on the quiet, moonlit surface of the lake of your mind when there is no breeze blowing.

15

A Sorcerer's Apprentice

Once upon a time there was a great Master who had a favorite disciple. The disciple served the Master for many many years aspiring to acquire the Master's knowledge. In the tradition we serve the masters and wait patiently for whatever little spark may come our way, whatever little spark we are qualified to receive or empowered to hold lest we get burnt.

One day the Master was very pleased with his disciple. He said to the disciple, "I will teach you a secret charm." "Finally, my Master will teach me something," he thought. "Now, listen, this is the charm with a secret word and the power of this charm is that as soon as you utter it, a great giant will appear before you, will bow down to you and say, 'How may I serve you, my Master?' But I have not taught you everything as yet. There are a number of controls that you have yet to learn. Do not go and start using this charm until you have learnt the controls, all right? Otherwise you could get into terrible dangers."

"Yes, Master," the student responded, "I wouldn't dream of doing such a thing without your express permission."

Like the sorcerer's apprentice, the young man could not wait to leave the Master's presence. He went to his house in the village, got into his courtyard, and stood there.

"Danger, what danger?", he thought. "My Master is always trying to frighten me. I would like to see the giant come and serve me."

He uttered the charm and there before him stood a great big giant, bowing down and saying, "How may I serve you, Master?"

And the disciple's mouth dropped open. "You came!"

"Didn't you call me, Master? You called me; I came."

"Oh, I was just trying it out. I don't really have much use for you. If the Master finds out, he will be very angry with me. Go away now."

"Go away? Well, then send me away."

"I am sending you away. Go away."

And the giant said, "Master, you should know I don't go away just like that. Whoever taught you to call me must have taught you some controls so that you could send me away."

"Oh well, I suppose I made a mistake. Can't you just go away? I don't have any need of you."

"No, when you call me, I come here to serve you."

"Well, all right, I have a few things you could do."

"You must have been taught that when you call me, there are one or two rules. One is that you have to keep me busy—keep giving me something to do at all times. The moment you have nothing for me to do, Master, I mean no harm, but I get pretty hungry because it is built into my nature. I normally begin to satisfy my hunger with eating my master. Sorry about that but that's the way it is!"

"Oh, oh, that's what he was talking about—the controls! All right, then, cook my meals, give me a bath, set the table, stand here and wait on me."

When the disciple issued the orders the giant carried them

out in no time.

"Now I am tired. It has been quite a day. Make me a bed." So the giant also made the bed for the disciple to rest.

"Well, Giant, I think I'm going to turn in and take a nap. Why don't you do the same? Rest."

"Rest?!! I told you I don't rest."

"Giant, I am tired. You have to let me rest. Now go away. Please go away."

"I am getting a little hungry," said the giant.

So the disciple who had been pretending to be a master over the giant, now began running at his fastest pace toward the woods where the Master lived and the giant strode confidently behind. In the vicinity of the hermitage, the disciple started to shout. "Help, help! Help, help!"

The Master was deep in *samadhi* and when one is in deep meditation sometimes to call him is like trying to penetrate something impenetrable like a rock. The Master wondered, "Is someone calling from some place for help or is it some *samskara* of mine arising? Let me check . . . . Oh, these people from the village! They won't let someone meditate without shouting, "help, help, help."

With great effort, the Master opened his eyes, rose to his feet, walked over and opened the door. There was his disciple, dear and trusted, falling into his arms.

"Master, Master, help, help."

"What's the matter? What happened?", asked the Master.

"The g-i-a-n-t!" said the trembling disciple.

"The giant?"

"Hurry, Master, protect me this one time. I'll do anything. I'll go through any penance. I'm sorry."

"All right. This one time, O.K. But don't do it again."

"No, Master, I won't."

The Master whispered something into the disciple's ear

and the disciple beamed. He turned confidently around and said to the giant, "I have something for you to do."

"I meant you no harm, Master, you know that. Just keep me busy."

"All right. Put me on your shoulder," ordered the disciple. The giant picked him up and put him on his shoulder. Back to the village they went.

"Put me down," he ordered. And the giant put him down.

"Now, Giant, what I want you to do is go into the forest and find a strong, straight, tall tree. Strip it of its twigs and branches and make one tall pole out of it. Fetch the pole on your shoulders and come down that hill."

The giant went into the forest and found a strong, straight, tall tree. He knocked off all the branches and twigs, prepared it as a pole, put it on his shoulders, and went down into the village.

"Here, Master."

"All right. Good. Now dig a deep hole in the ground. Put the trunk in the ground. Put sod around. Is the pole straight and firm?"

"Yes, it is straight and firm, Master."

"Now go and get me a strong rope."

The giant found a strong rope.

"Now tie this end of the rope to the top of the pole." The giant did so.

"Now, Giant, hold this end of the rope and climb up."

He climbed up.

"Climb down." He climbed down.

"Climb up. Come down. Climb up. Come down. Up. Down. Up. Down." went the disciple.

"Good, Giant. Keep doing that until I have something else for you to do!", said the disciple with glee, now in command of the giant.

The giant is the mind. Without anything specific for the mind to do, it gets pretty hungry. It turns on you and devours you. The straight pole firmly set on the ground is your spine. The rope is the thread of your breath. Set your spine firmly straight on the ground, hold on to the thread of your breath and with that go up and down and up and down, up and down on the path of the *Kundalini.*

Mantra is the control that the guru was going to teach the disciple. May your mantra control the giant called the mind.

Further Readings Recommended

Arthur Avalon, *Serpent Power,* Ganesh & Co., Madras, India, several editions.

Arthur Avalon, *The Garland of Letters,* Ganesh & Co., Madras, India, several editions.

Swami Pratyagatmananda Saraswati, *Japa-sutram,* 6 vols. Ganesh & Co., Madras, India.

Appendix

Photographs Showing the Use of the Mala

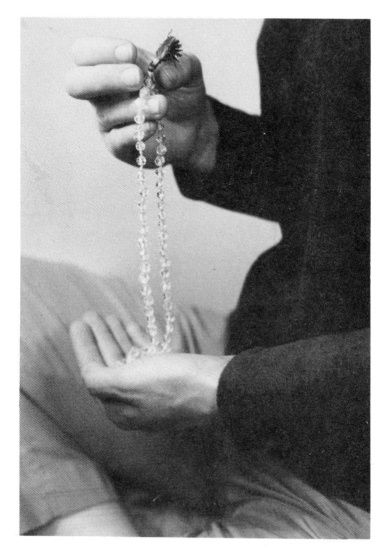

positioning mala on ring finger

using mala

mala at heart center

mala at heart center (side view)

coming to the end of a round (A)

rotating mala around guru bead (B)

repositioning fingers after rotating (C)

beginning next round (D)

The main building of the national headquarters, Honesdale, Pa.

The Himalayan Institute

Since its establishment in 1971, the Himalayan Institute has been dedicated to helping individuals develop themselves physically, mentally, and spiritually, as well as contributing to the transformation of society. All the Institute programs—educational, therapeutic, research—emphasize holistic health, yoga, and meditation as tools to help achieve those goals. Institute programs combine the best of ancient wisdom and modern science, of Eastern teachings and Western technologies. We invite you to join with us in this ongoing process of personal growth and development.

Our beautiful national headquarters, on a wooded 400-acre campus in the Pocono Mountains of northeastern Pennsylvania, provides a peaceful, healthy setting for our seminars, classes, and training programs in the principles and practices of holistic living. Students from around the world have joined us here to attend programs in such diverse areas as biofeedback and stress reduction, hatha yoga, meditation, diet and nutrition, philosophy and metaphysics, and practical psychology for better living. We see the realization of our human potentials as a lifelong quest, leading to increased health, creativity, happiness, awareness, and improving the quality of life.

The Institute is a nonprofit organization. Your membership in the Institute helps to support its programs. Please call or write for information on becoming a member.

Institute Programs, Services, and Facilities

All Institute programs share an emphasis on conscious, holistic living and personal self-development. You may enjoy any of a number of diverse programs, including:

• Special weekend or extended seminars to teach skills and techniques for increasing your ability to be healthy and enjoy life

• Holistic health services

• Professional training for health professionals

• Meditation retreats and advanced meditation instruction

• Cooking and nutritional training

• Hatha yoga and exercise workshops

• Residential programs for self-development

The Himalayan Institute Charitable Hospital

A major aspect of the Institute's work around the world is its support of the construction and management of a modern, comprehensive hospital and holistic health facility in the mountain area of Dehra Dun, India. Outpatient facilities are already providing medical care to those in need, and mobile units have been equipped to visit outlying villages. Construction work on the main hospital building is progressing as scheduled.

We welcome financial support to help with the construction and the provision of services. We also welcome donations of medical supplies, equipment, or professional expertise. If you would like further information on the Hospital, please contact us.